SUFFERING AND THE
COURAGE OF GOD

SUFFERING AND THE
COURAGE OF GOD
Exploring How Grace and Suffering Meet

ROBERT CORIN MORRIS

PARACLETE PRESS
BREWSTER, MASSACHUSETTS

Library of Congress Cataloging-in-Publication Data
Morris, Robert Corin, 1941-
  Suffering and the courage of God : exploring how grace and suffering meet / by Robert Corin Morris.
        p. cm.
  ISBN 1-55725-428-1
  1. Suffering—Religious aspects—Christianity. 2. Grace (Theology) I. Title.
BV4909.M668 2005
231'.8—dc22   2005012932

10 9 8 7 6 5 4 3 2 1

Published by Paraclete Press
Brewster, Massachusetts
www.paracletepress.com

Printed in the United States of America

CONTENTS

PART ONE
the challenge of suffering

INTRODUCTION
out of the prison

ODDLY ENOUGH, THE WAY OF OUT of my suffering came only when I accepted that there might be no way out of it—that I might have to live with the pain I was carrying for the rest of my life. Little did I realize the doors such acceptance might open.

Suffering can come in many forms, small and great. But how we deal with it begins with our response to whatever life presents us, from minor inconveniences to major tragedies. Life slowly taught me that the way we deal with each difficulty either intensifies the suffering or opens doors to its redemption. In my case, it took a great adversity to teach me how to deal with the small ones.

The suffering I faced in my mid-forties was emotional, but cripplingly real nonetheless. Behind the surface of an outwardly productive and seemingly successful life as a priest in a suburban Episcopal parish, a persistent low-grade pain hummed silently in the background of my soul, the bitter fruit of a childhood of periodic emotional scarring. My father's violent temper and my mother's alternating episodes of intense rage and expressive love had left deeper scars on my psyche than I had previously realized. I began to notice how much I was using my otherwise worthy activities as a pastor, husband, colleague, and friend—preaching, teaching, team projects, spiritual practice, interesting conversations, heartwarming films, good books, even friendship and marriage themselves—as ways to escape this pain. Every time I really came "home" to myself, there it was, quietly throbbing, sending me out once again to find some new diversion from the discomfort. Not only that, but as my awareness of this background pain surfaced, I noticed how often it flared when I felt personally wounded by someone. What I had identified as periods of wanting to withdraw and close myself down now began painting themselves in more vivid colors as occasions when some outer event hit the raw wound of past emotional abuse, causing an overreaction to otherwise minor incidents. Each new venture gave me a soothing thrill of pleasure, but did little to heal the pain within.

This was all the more discouraging because I had already spent the decade of my thirties finding some relief from my own bipolar depressive illness, (a legacy from my mother's genes, and the unsuspected cause of her alternating moods).[1] That biologically based disease had been like a roller coaster, sending me reeling from the depths to the heights at least once a year. I had understood this as a personal, psychological flaw until receiving proper diagnosis and treatment. I'll discuss my recovery from that disease later on in this book, but for now suffice it to say that through the decade of that struggle I had hoped emotional turmoil would someday find a simple, peaceful resolution, and my suffering would cease. Now, it seemed, the gradual but real remission of the bipolar depression through therapy and medicine had merely cleared the ground for this deeper, underlying distress to emerge. I was now presented with a real psychological problem that had been hiding behind the disease.

I felt inwardly trapped. I had tried every "fix" available. Sadly, it seemed, I had run out of options. Maybe I would have to live with this hum of pain for the rest of my life. Would I do that? Could I do that?

The facts of my life were confronting me, not for the first time, with a harsh choice: Will you face the facts as they are, or will you keep trying to escape them? Do you have the courage to carry this pain to the grave, if need be, or will you spend your time mourning a healing that hasn't happened? Is the already significant good in your life satisfying enough to accept this persistent pain as one part of the total package? Can you live thankfully, enjoying what you have?

Being out of alternatives, this seemed an offer I couldn't refuse, so I said to myself, to life itself, and to God, "Okay, okay, okay. If that's the choice, I choose life, as it is, even though some part of me is still in the prison of this pain." Although I had made this choice, I found this question still dangling: *How* could I accept this pain without remaining its victim? Where could I find the courage to make this possible?

Paradoxically, it is often our unwillingness to accept the way things are that blocks any possibility of future change. Having accepted that I might live with this pain forever, I was soon invited to a fresh exploration of possibilities.

I had a dream: Trapped in a prison cell, I gripped the bars, looking into the mournful eyes of an abused, suffering Christ who stood just outside my cage. This was an absolutely stereotypical, stained-glass image of Jesus as archetypal victim: crown of thorns, red robe, patient, sad and long-suffering countenance.

My first response was to recoil. I was in the midst of rebellion against my own particular childhood image of Christ, which was based on a dark strain of Christian piety that sees suffering as a good thing, in and of itself. The abused child in me had identified with Jesus as the "good kid" who accepts his abuse patiently and passively. Jesus was the best kid ever. No wonder the bullies went after him, the archetypal scapegoat, the perfect victim. The particular strain of fundamentalism in which I was raised emphasized, perversely, that the greater the suffering, the greater the good for all—like the child in an abusive family, unconsciously targeted as the scapegoat, whose suffering benefits those who can unload their frustrations on him, rather than having to bear their own emotional turmoil. This had been the original, albeit unwitting, framework of meaning for my own suffering.

Something healthy in me had long since rejected this version of Jesus, finding in Scripture a more robust and life-giving person. So why was this abject figure standing in front of my prison cell? "Get me out of here," I begged. The mournful face broke into a kindly smile, and the eyes suddenly revealed a surprisingly strong resilience—a love that had courageously endured deep suffering, yet not been undone by it. "The cell door isn't really locked," he said. "Go on, push it open. You can leave if you want to." And then he disappeared. My dream self pushed on the cell door. It opened. I stood in the cell, astonished, wondering what to do next as I awoke.

No miracle cure came along with this dream, but I knew it was an invitation to learn how to deal with my suffering differently. The subtle transformation of Christ's face from the sadness of suffering to the strength of courageous love invited me to see him in a new way. Somehow, the way out of the prison had to do with learning to see that suffering differently. What was Jesus' own way of dealing with suffering?

I can't claim to have penetrated the heart of God on this matter, but as I'll soon relate, I came to see the suffering Christ not as a helpless victim but as a subtle victor, courageously engaged in a deep struggle against the power of any victimizing force to undo us. His suffering is not borne passively, but embraced actively by a love and life bigger than any suffering—God's own eternally springing life, manifest in Christ, available to all, whether the external forms of adversity change or not. As I came to see this courageous Christ in a fresh light, I began both to realize and believe that all our sufferings are carried in an even bigger and stronger courage—God's own courageous love. This vast life, from which we cannot be separated, enters into all the difficulties creatures face with abundant grace to help us overcome all the power that would trap us in a prison house of fear, resignation, and helplessness.

Astonished at the very idea that my own courage could be rooted in a courage as deep as God's—an idea we will explore in more depth in the next chapter—I was able to embrace my inward hum of pain instead of running from it, working through it step by step in a healing process that has gone farther than I initially dared to imagine. While some inner scar tissue can be jolted into a dull hurting, the persistent low hum has long since departed.

This book comes out of many years of discovery and transformation that made me more compassionate with myself and those to whom I minister, as we all seek the courage to face adversity in ways that lessen, rather than add to the suffering of the world. Everything I've written comes not only from what I learned in my own experience, but even more from hearing the stories of how other people deal courageously with their own difficulties. All this has changed the way I approach even minor annoyances. I hope the witness of these lives, and my own personal insights, may offer some help in opening the seemingly locked doors in others' lives.

CHAPTER ONE
when suffering comes

SUFFERING NEVER SAVED ANYBODY. Not your suffering. Not mine. Not even Jesus' suffering saves, in and of itself. Rather, so far as I have seen it in my own experience and that of others, it is the *way* suffering is faced that makes the difference between whether pain, sorrow, difficulty, deprivation, or challenge becomes part of our self's stretching or shrinking. Suffering is a challenge—a gauntlet thrown in our path. When faced with adversity, we must make a choice.

One family is sideswiped by the unexpected birth of a child with a catastrophic handicap, and everyone draws together in mutual support. After the inevitable shock and grief, they decide to accept the cards dealt to them by circumstance, and embrace this child, with all its difficulties. In so doing, their hearts are stretched: "It's changed our expectations about what's important in life," the father says.

Another couple greets an infant with an even lesser handicap with a resistant bitterness. So set are they on their expectations of happiness that this unwanted accident of nature cannot be absorbed. "It's like our lives were supposed to end up in southern California and we got hijacked to the Arctic Circle! We don't want to be in this situation. It wasn't what we had our hearts set on." The baby is put in an institution, but the wound to the dream endures, unhealed. Eventually the couple separates, their marriage relationship too strained to bear the enormity of this whiplash.

We don't have to believe that God causes suffering—and I don't—to recognize that adversity can put us into what the Bible calls "the Test"—that crucible of choice that tests our mettle and demands life-changing decisions.[2] Life, sooner or later, is difficult for every person—not all the time, but from time to time, even for those in fortunate circumstances.[3] Those difficult times do, indeed, test our mettle. In them character is formed or weakened. Like it or not, this is the way life sometimes is.

Both families faced shock, disappointment, grief, and understandable railing against their fate. But the way they dealt with their suffering was quite different. While both couples deserve our sympathy and compassionate understanding, it is clear that the outcomes were very different because the choices made were different.

The word "suffering" may bring to mind dramatic events, like car accidents, life threatening disease, natural disaster, or personal injury. But how we deal with suffering begins with how we choose to respond to the stuff of any ordinary day. The yolks may break as I am preparing sunny-side up eggs for breakfast; I may get stuck in a traffic jam; phone calls and e-mails may conspire to keep me from doing my work; my spouse may be in a bad mood when I get home; and the light bulb in the reading lamp may burn out just as I am finally settling down to read the daily paper. Each of these events is potentially a moment of suffering, depending on how we deal with it. There are people who are able to turn the ordinary inconveniences of everyday life into major occasions for misery. Others seem able to bear with life's rough edges in a way that deepens their resilience and softens the rough edges of their souls—their essential selves. The quality of daily life is made more sweet or sour by how we deal with every such occurrence. Over a lifetime, these daily habits actually shape how we see the world.

lamenters or life-embracers?

We've all known people who become hardened and embittered by their difficulties or disabilities. In my first year of ministry I took home communions to over thirty elderly shut-ins each month. Some of them were stuck, miserable, victims of their circumstances. Their chief lament was how unsympathetic people were to their plight; but sympathy, no matter how constant, seemed to disappear into a bottomless pit. Much as one might have compassion for them, their continual complaints had become off-putting to friends and family alike.

In my youthful inexperience I wondered, fearfully, if this bitterness was what old age threatened for all of us. I was saved from this conclusion by another group of shut-ins, equally challenged, who spoke in simple acceptance of their limitations and with quiet gratitude about their lives. I came to learn that they had undergone deep inner struggle to find acceptance and gratitude, passing through their own moments of resistance, nights of anger, days of sorrow, and bursts of outrage, coming to final acceptance and, with it, the power to live gracefully, embracing life as it came to them.

The life circumstances of the situation-resistant lamenters had not been significantly different from those of the quietly thankful life-embracers. Both suffered, but in wholly different worlds. The thankful ones saw life as a series of challenges to be faced. Adversity was something to be accepted, dealt with, lived through, learned from, and redeemed. The victims saw life as a tale of repeated, undeserved woe. Beset and besieged in a world of endless trials foisted upon them by the mysterious malignity of life itself, they had shrunk into private, inner hells. For most of their lives they had met every difficulty with resistance, persistent resentment, and accumulating outrage.

Suffering, in and of itself, can be an easy route through outrage to evil. Embittered by suffering, we may begin to lash out at others. I suffer, so why should you be happy? You do me an injury, so I strike back. Your ancestors were unjust to mine; I live in resentment, waiting for revenge.

Such struggles are the most difficult moments of human life. We're pushed, sometimes brutally, up against the rough edges of our own souls. The heart and mind can be stunned, shaken, and thrown into a terrible crisis of meaning. We may discover emotional depths and attitudes we never imagined we had. Tough inner choices are demanded. Will we hide? Face the situation? Succumb to guilt? Be swept away by fear? Hate life? Blame God?

I know from my own harsh struggles with depression and emotional pain that it's not the place of anyone outside the skin of the afflicted person to judge people harshly who succumb to the bitterness of suffering. We can't know what's going on in the mystery of their hearts—what childhood fears or adult beliefs, inner emotional pits or intellectual barriers keep them from facing their suffering differently. I know from the many times I've postponed dealing with a difficulty how powerful such inner forces can be, and I cannot afford to deliver ultimate judgments about anyone else.

But the brute fact of life is that different choices mean different outcomes. Those who survive and grow more resilient in times of suffering have found the spiritual resources of acceptance, endurance, and patience to deal with their trials, whatever the outcome. Such acceptance often leads to gratitude and compassion. They face life with enlarged hearts.

So much depends on which state of heart and mind meets, endures, and responds to the adversity. Do we undergo it as a prison house of assaults and betrayals, or do we somehow find a more spacious inner state that reaches out for the goodness of life in spite of the suffering?

The first time I saw this dramatically lived out was in a woman in her late seventies, to whom life had dealt a terrible blow. The person I'll call Myrtle had good reasons for her resentments. Her son, her only son whom she loved, had died tragically in mid-life, leaving behind a wife and family. Distraught with grief, Myrtle had "lost consciousness" while driving to church one dreary Sunday morning and rammed her car into a telephone pole. Miraculously, she survived life-threatening injuries, and after three months of hospital recovery, was home. Only one problem lingered: occasional shooting pains in her leg. But to make matters worse, her husband had developed a painful case of shingles just at the moment she needed his help. Her exasperation at him was only making his condition worse. The inner walls of victimhood were closing in. After a quiet tirade about every aspect of her existence, including her husband's betrayal of her through his illness, she blinked, looked at me, and asked tremulously, "Do you think I'm becoming a terrible harpy?"

Well, truth be told, she was, most of all to her unfortunate husband. I blinked, swallowed hard, and sent off an inward prayer for guidance. What should I, as a pastor, say to this poor, life-battered woman? Murmur sympathy, as I had for months, or tell her the honest truth? I followed the guidance that came back in answer to my prayer: As gently as possible, I told her that she was, indeed, headed straight for harpydom. I said I understood she had lots of good reasons for it, and that no one could blame her if she did. But did she really want to end up in that kind of inner hell, however good the causes for it might be?

Tearfully, she confessed that she felt terrible about her complaining spirit. But what was she to do, especially with this continuing pain? My inner prayers for guidance became intensified, and I heard myself saying, "Well, Jesus tells us to love our enemies, and bless those who curse us. The pain is now a deadly enemy of your soul, not just your body. Every time it comes, why don't you bless it instead of cursing it?" I myself had been pondering Jesus' challenge in the Sermon on the Mount, to "bless, not curse" recently, about a wholly different matter, and, as it turned out, by the grace of God the idea was ready at hand in that moment for Myrtle's situation.[4]

Grace of God or not, part of me was horrified to face this poor, suffering woman with such a rigorous demand. Yet that was what had come in answer to my prayer, so, reluctantly, I said it. To my everlasting surprise and relief, Myrtle gasped, sat up straight, dried her eyes, pursed her lips in thought for a minute and then said, quite matter-of-factly, "Very well, then; that's what I'll do." And so she did. She arose, cared for her husband, and blessed her pain, which slowly receded over the coming weeks. Most importantly, her spirits turned toward accepting her life as it was, with blessing rather than cursing. In the midst of suffering, she had ceased to be its victim.

redemptive suffering—or suffering redemptively?

Christians often speak loosely about *"redemptive suffering,"* as if suffering itself had some curative value. Suffering itself was not ennobling Myrtle, but embittering her.

It is more helpful, I believe, to speak of *suffering redemptively*. By this I mean facing suffering with a courage and compassion that can clear our minds for creative responses to adversity. This is not a mere quibble over words. The way we speak of things shapes our beliefs and expectations. To call suffering itself redemptive is to suggest that just to experience adversity, pain, abuse, and oppression contains some hidden divine energy for good.

Life had faced Myrtle with a choice about how she would respond to the harsh side of existence. Encouraged to trust in the wisdom of Jesus, she chose to face her sufferings differently. Rather than letting the suffering define or rule her, she called upon a resource from beyond the suffering: the power of blessing, which began to transform her experience. She learned how to suffer redemptively, instead of expecting that suffering itself would "make her better."

There is nothing in the Gospels to suggest that Jesus ever deliberately sought suffering, or encouraged others to seek it. Indeed, he seems to do everything possible to alleviate it: healing the sick, forgiving troubled sinners, reconciling the outcast, and comforting the sorrowful, challenging the powers of oppression. Adversaries begin to stalk him, yes: Slanders from fearful opponents are hurled, and a growing threat of arrest looms over him. But this opposition is because his zeal for the burning vision of the kingdom—the rule of God's grace in human life—makes him the enemy of all that causes unnecessary suffering, inwardly or outwardly. That opposition will lead to the suffering of the cross, and yet on the verge of his arrest, he still prays "earnestly" to be delivered from that ordeal if there is another way to accomplish God's purposes for his life. By the time he rises from his prayer, he is able to approach what seems like crushing defeat in such a way that it becomes a path to victory.

Making this distinction between Christ's redemptive way of meeting suffering and suffering itself is crucial. Psychological health and spiritual wholeness demand a refusal to choose the path of helplessness and victimhood—even if we are actually being victimized. That path opens us to a dark, masochistic undercurrent that many forms of spirituality cultivate by seeing a spiritual power in pain itself.

Primitive beliefs all over the world see self-inflicted punishment as a way to get the attention of the Spirit or spirits. The more pain the better. The priests of Ba'al, in their contest with Elijah on Mount Carmel, "cut themselves with swords and lances until the blood gushed out over them."[5] Various shamanic ceremonies involve self-inflicted pain to raise spiritual energy. Celtic Christian monks stood waist-deep in cold winter water, and countless thousands of medieval Christians wore hair shirts, lashed themselves with whips, or mixed ashes in their food to subdue the passions of the flesh and "share the sufferings" of Christ.

"Sharing in Christ's sufferings" is not about self-inflicted pain, whatever use such practices may have in toughening the body and refining the whole self. We share in Christ's sufferings when we pursue, in spite of opposition, his vision of the kingdom, God's desire for earthly life, when we participate in Christ's way of meeting suffering and its sources. We also follow the way of the cross when we meet the natural adversities of the world—sickness, hardship, adversity—in the Spirit that Christ manifests. This means facing any adversity, whatever its cause, emulating Christ's way of suffering redemptively.

facing the opposition within

That way involves facing not only the adversity that attacks from outside us, but the resistance that arises from within us. When life does not go as we expect it to, frustration, impatience, and disappointment may be our first and natural reaction. But if we do not work with things as they are, such reactions may deepen into resentment and a feeling of helplessness. With repeated disappointments, self-pity and even self-loathing may set in.

It's even possible to begin subtly enjoying the "secondary gains" that may accrue to the sufferer: special attention, some lessening of ordinary demands. We may find, however unconsciously, positive advantages in the familiar companionship of suffering.

A friend I'll call Valerie realized how far she'd gone down this beguiling path when she was healed from the partial immobility imposed by the severe bursitis in her right shoulder. Medical treatments had failed to relieve the problem. Right-handed, Valerie learned how to use her left hand for most tasks. Not consciously happy about her condition at all, she faced her handicap with good humor, making do with her left hand when she could, and asking for help when she couldn't.

One day a friend offered to take her to a prayer meeting being led by a "remarkable healer." Valerie dismissed the invitation at first. She wasn't interested in anything "fringe" or "far out," and was a bit skeptical about allegedly remarkable healers. Still, if it might help . . . So she went—and was healed!

Astonished and joyful, she returned to her ordinary tasks. A couple of days after the healing, putting groceries away pleasurably with her right hand on the top shelf, she "was hit by a wave of grief that stopped me in my tracks. I actually missed my disability, as if I had lost my closest companion. More startlingly, part of me wanted it back." A bit baffled, she noted her reaction, realized she faced an inner resistance to her healing, chose not to accept its invitation, and continued putting the groceries away, thankful for her recovery.

Each "small" step like Valerie's we take in dealing with our sufferings bravely is a victory, making us more fit to cope with this life, and more able to participate in the world-redeeming life and love of God that surrounds us, and into which, I believe, we continue to grow after death. By resisting the dark current of masochism and the cultivation of secondary gain which can imprison us in victimhood, she tasted in her own small way Christ's path of victory.

Christ—abused victim or courageous warrior?

It took me a long time to see how that victory was won. Certainly Easter Sunday came every year, and with it trumpet blasts of victory, but it always seemed strangely disconnected from Good Friday. On that dark day, I saw the Righteous One being beaten up by evil opponents. Then, two days later, the whole thing got mysteriously reversed, as if in reward for all his suffering. Somehow the suffering was supposed to be good, something God in fact willed to save us.

Nowhere did I see a Christ whose *way* of dealing with the rejection, betrayal, and pain of the Cross was victorious, itself a foreshadowing of the Easter triumph—a way of resilience rather than resignation, of courage and resistance to evil rather than blind submission to mystery. The Cross was presented as redemptive suffering itself, rather than as a clue to suffering redemptively. As I have already noted in the Introduction, I had been raised to see Christ as the battered Victim whose passive acceptance of abuse mysteriously redeems the world. In talking to many others over the years, I do not think I am alone in such impressions.[6] When I quipped once that I was baffled by why people didn't sit at the front of the church, a woman joked, "It's because of that cross up there. Nobody wants to get close to it." The good news of Jesus' triumphant way *through* suffering hadn't gotten through to her.

Slowly, over the years, a very different image of Christ has emerged from my pondering and praying, beginning with a very distinct inward vision during a Palm Sunday service the year my rebellion against Christ as the innocent, abused "good kid" reached its zenith. As I sat in church listening to the tale of the silent Jesus standing in the midst of his abusive enemies, I felt so sickened I seriously considered walking out on this apparent cult of pain and sorrow. How could this man be an example to anyone of health, healing, and salvation?

Instead of fleeing the church service, I fled to the inmost depths of my heart, and prayed for illumination. The answer came swift and clear: I saw the vast expanse of the starry sky, and these words echoed deep in my mind: "The one who has the midnight sky in his heart need fear no man." Then I inwardly saw Jesus standing silently before Pilate, and realized that the midnight sky was in his own heart, just as it can be in ours. He was not standing passively accepting abuse, but nobly, without fear, facing his enemy with courage and compassion, larger in soul than his opponents *because he was rooted in a goodness deeper than the suffering.* Even in the midst of suffering, the taproot of his spirit was deeply anchored in the goodness of God. I realized in that moment that this was a clue to Jesus' secret of facing life in this wild, wonderful, and terribly difficult universe.

Because Christ knows intimately the indestructible life of God within him, he can find the bravery to bear up under the worst that life can hurl at him, opening the darkest places of human life to the light of God. This God-rootedness makes it possible for him to find the courage and compassion to face the wilderness and the demons, the diseases and the betrayals, the fears and foes, and finally the dark realm of the dead itself, allowing the life of God itself to bear him up, bear him through. Even death itself is not to be feared, because every circumstance, whatever the cause, is a potential portal to the eternal reality of God's love which surrounds and sustains our own small lives.

This insight was reinforced on Good Friday as I read Psalm 22, traditionally associated with Christ, in which the sufferer's bones are out of joint, his hands pierced, his spirit poured out like water. Most amazingly, in the midst of all this suffering, he remembers the goodness of his mother's breast: "[I]t was you who took me from the womb; you kept me safe on my mother's breast."[7] In the midst of agony, the sufferer stays connected to a sense of goodness, rather than being pulled into the terrible vortex of fear, anger, helplessness, and grief that swirls in his heart. The suffering is met, received, and held in a heart still in touch with a goodness as deep and vast as the midnight sky.

finding the courage to care

This surrounding, sustaining goodness comes to us through many channels, for it is the divine grace itself. A caring friend takes under his wing a professional colleague who is battling emotional demons, listening to him over a weekly lunch. Fellow church members make sure an elderly widow is not left alone, setting up a group to read books to her. Someone practicing "random acts of kindness" gives a tollhouse cookie to a parkway toll agent who, unbeknownst to the giver, is having the worst day of his life—a simple act of human caring that turns him away from the brink of despair.

Or such goodness may come through the inner illuminations that arise through spiritual practice—darts of love that penetrate the confusion and complexity of our inner world with an image, or word, or insight that reorients us to life's goodness and expands the roominess of our world, a world that is always and everywhere overarched and overshadowed by the "midnight sky" of God's life and love. In later chapters, we'll discuss ways of cultivating this sense of goodness.

Being grounded, goodness is the basis for the courage we need to face adversity, for courage can arise only when we care about something enough to defend and protect it—in this case, the love of life itself and our willingness to invest ourselves in it. Only so can we survive suffering, and if possible, seek ways to cure or challenge its causes.

A suffering world is not saved by agonizing over it. That only adds to the suffering. The world is saved by love of the good and the bravery to preserve and increase it, by a courageous compassion that faces adversity and moves forward, looking for whatever goodness is possible in any situation. Jesus faces the evil actions of his opponents—and his own inner opposition—like a martial arts master in combat, like a doctor wrestling with cancer, or a therapist up against a patient's suicidal impulse: alert, caring, nimble, and savvy to outfox and outwit the dark enemies of life's goodness with sanity, compassion, and confidence in the power of the good to endure and triumph. His wounds are not the sign that suffering is good, but that some things in life are good enough to suffer for. They are the wounds of a brave warrior bloodied in the fight to free those who have gotten lost in the prison house of suffering, as we will see further in Chapter Two.

Christ's way of suffering redemptively models the courage that can grow us strong, caring, and supple as we face any adversity. For Christ, for us, and for everyone who has found such courage in the midst of adversity, the source of victory is the same: God's own courage in the midst of a world of dazzling beauty, soul-sustaining goodness, and sometimes terrifying adversity.

For a way to open yourself to the "midnight sky" of God's love and simply being present to God, see Prayer Exercises 1 and 2 in the Appendix.

the courage of God

IF COURAGE ITSELF BEGINS IN THE HEART of God, then finding our connection to it can empower us as we face difficulty, danger, or simple daily challenges in the wildly magnificent beauty, challenge, and possibility of this world. We do not usually think of God as needing courage. Isn't God too big and powerful, the source, creator, and sustainer of all that is? Surely, God has absolute mastery and control. What need is there for courage?

And yet, many biblical stories that witness to how divine grace works imply courage again and again. God is pictured in the roles of creator, parent, lover, and warrior, each of which involves risk-taking—which, in turn, requires courage.

The Bible uses down-to-earth stories to talk about God, rather than some direct, clinical description of the Mystery that underlies all reality. Each tale reveals different qualities of the divine presence in the world: the healing love that cures a leper, the justice that overthrows an oppressive ruler, the endurance that sustains the suffering poor, and the companionship that embraces the solitary sufferer. These divine attributes are then celebrated in prayer and song, such as Psalm 145's declaration that "The Lord is gracious and merciful, slow to anger and abounding in steadfast love."[8]

The usual list of divine attributes is a familiar one: love, justice, compassion, forgiveness, creativity, and caring, to name but a few. Courage has not, traditionally, been on the list. But it's there silently, like gravity in the universe, fundamental to all else. "Courage is the foundation that underlies and gives reality to all other virtues and personal values," says the existential psychologist Rollo May. "Courage is necessary to make being and becoming possible."[9] All reality is rooted in this divine courage-to-be, God's bravery to participate fully in the wonder and challenge of the universe.

story—the nature of biblical language

What the inner life of God is like, of course, is ultimately a mystery to us. After all, we don't entirely know the mystery of our own inner life! Forbidden as we are to make graven images, we dare not worship the metaphors of God made in our own emotional image, or absolutize even the scriptural images. But these same Scriptures do not hesitate to use boldly human language to reveal the indescribable Mystery. In the stories, God falls in love, likes some people specially, laughs, frowns, rejoices, gets angry, plots punishment, repents of the plot, makes promises, and sometimes seems to break them.[10]

Many modern readers see in such language only crude primitivism, the reduction of God to human attributes—some of them humanity's worst at that! But though we are always in danger of thinking God is just a bigger version of ourselves, the scriptural language suggests that human nature is *theomorphic*, God-shaped, rather than that God is *anthropomorphic* or human-shaped. The ancient commentators saw this clearly, as when the great, second-century Alexandrine teacher Origen called such language *anthropathic*—literally "human-feeling"—because God is "assuming the manners" of human beings to communicate to human hearts. For example, the "'wrath' of God is to be understood figuratively . . . for it is as if one were to call the words of a physician 'threats,' when he tells his patients, 'I will have to use the knife and apply cauteries if you do not obey my prescriptions.'"[11]

Origen echoed the earlier rabbinical and apostolic teaching that these stories are "for our instruction."[12] In them, Divinity stoops to our condition, translating the movements of its vast heart into human terms so that we can not only understand but also emulate them. The themes of our adoration are meant to be the practice our lives. Each story has a "moral level" of meaning beyond the literal, calling us, as Paul says, to "grow up in every way" by learning how to act in accordance with all the attributes of the image of God at the core of our being, the root of all our capacities.[13]

The stories call forth the image of God in us. Reading a story of how God thinks upon mercy even in the midst of wrath, we can grow our own anger beyond its reactive smoke into a holy flame of loving opposition to all that twists and spoils human life, seeking to "overcome evil by good."[14] God's grace and mercy call forth our own. So also, to believe in divine courage reassures us that our own courage is rooted in an inexhaustible bravery.

but isn't God beyond it all?

In spite of the vividness of the biblical narrative, there are those who would say that courage is an inappropriate attribute for God. Surely God is transcendent, invulnerable, above it all. Such an objection comes much more from conventional theology than from the heart of the biblical revelation. Such teachings arose under the influence of Greek culture, which reinterpreted the vivid, parable-like language of the Bible in the abstract categories of Hellenistic philosophy. Pagan wisdom postulated a God who was not only transcendent but "impassible," unable to be influenced, acted upon, or affected by anything lesser—invulnerable. In such conventional teaching, God's transcendence is taken to mean that God sees our suffering from "above," offering sympathy and help, but not trapped in the midst of it like the rest of us. To be human is to be limited; to be divine unfettered, free, and clear of all earth's turbulent change.

Such invulnerable Divinity is a far cry from the passionate, highly expressive God pictured in the Bible—and is a bit remote from the acute pain of a bone cancer sufferer or a grieving spouse. This heavenly controller of all just doesn't have to endure the anguish of creation the way we do. The result of such teaching can be the bitterness with which an aged widower, grieving the sudden death of a beloved wife, said to me, "Why does God put us through this? Are we just some kind of experiment, like rats in a maze?" Such suspicions are not uncommon in popular belief, though they are rarely admitted.

The God of Scripture, however, says, "In their afflictions, I am afflicted."[15] Can we honor the essence of this historical impassibility doctrine and still accept the biblical Good News that the Divine enters, with us, into all the challenges of life as a full participant? My answer came with that Palm Sunday's "midnight sky" revelation that I shared in Chapter One: The depth and vastness of God's life is bigger than any of the suffering included in it. In technical theological terms, God is both transcendent and immanent, transcending suffering even while participating in it to redeem it.

As my seminary tutor and long-time friend Dr. Fred Shriver puts it, "There's got to be a place where all this suffering stops. That's what the impassibility doctrine is getting at." Wholly involved in our suffering, God is vaster than the narrow confines of it. In the depths of the divine Life is an unquenchable joy that transcends, surrounds, and sustains us in our suffering. Made in God's image, we, too, have our own capacity for transcendence, an ability of the psyche to "go beyond" the boundary of our suffering and breathe the air of a larger life. Communing with this divine Life gives space for the courage needed to deal with adversity.

the courage to create

If we wish to see the divine courage in action, we do best to let the stories speak for themselves. Consider creation itself. The great prose poem that opens Genesis is so bedazzling in its grandeur that we may miss the edge of fearful delight that underlies it. God repeatedly speaks matters into motion, but waits each time to behold creation as it cascades out of the dark nothingness of chaos like fruit from a cornucopia. Dark waters begin to shine with the dawning of the first light, seas swirl and separate so dry land can emerge, the waters, earth, and air begin to swarm with new life. After each enormous day of creation, God *sees* that it is *tov*—a Hebrew word meaning good, delightful, pleasurable, utterly "delectable." This sounds more like the delight of a novice cook who, a bit on edge about the outcome, has peeked through the oven window at her fragile soufflé in the oven to see if it's "coming out right," than someone who has it all down pat in advance.

The fertile chaos of the first moment of any creation always lurks, ready to assert itself again. The creative process isn't entirely predictable. The potter envisions the pot, yes; but the clay has ideas of its own. The author has a plot in mind, but the imagined characters in the novel may suddenly begin behaving in unexpected ways. However clear the initial vision, the actual process will involve surprises, unanticipated developments, and repeated readjustments. As the creative process deepens, the creation takes on a life of its own, and the process becomes an emerging dialogue, even power struggle, between creator and creation. Will the soufflé, pot, or novel come out "very good" in the end or not? Creativity is a leap into the unknown, requiring courage, because it lets loose forces that are not entirely controllable.

In the biblical story, creation does begin taking on "a life of its own." Even though all is of God and from God, there is a hint in the story that creation is, partly, a cooperative event. God doesn't so much create directly as call creation forth from the dark depths of the deep chaos. The earth "brings forth" in response to the divine call, implying cooperation. Other creation narratives amplify this sense of partnership by picturing God assisted by Wisdom as a "master worker," while the morning stars "sing for joy."[16]

The need for courage culminates in the creation of "earthlings"— human beings gifted with godlike abilities to be the stewards and developers of creation, including the ability to make choices.[17] The "humanity project" that will form the backbone of the biblical saga is born. God has launched the creation venture, but entrusts a major part of it to these new and untested creatures. The whole Story from now on will be about God's ventures with a creation rife with unpredictable freedom. "God's power is plenipotentiary, not controlling," my friend Mark says. That means God's power is always able to deal with the unpredictable, even the rebellious and wayward, in ways that work every event toward God's good purposes. And a good thing, too, for as the Story goes, God encounters angels who rebel, a serpent that connives, and godlike humans who mishandle their God-given opportunities.

the courage to parent

The gift of human freedom leads to heartbreaking consequences for the very One who birthed it. Brother kills brother, and violence spreads. The wonderful gift of creativity is devoted to destruction: "Their heart's planning was only evil all the day ". The breathtaking beauty of creation is marred, its deftly interwoven fabric torn by humanity. The brutally intense words of the Hebrew original describe a dire situation: Humanity has "ruined its way upon earth." In a poignant echo of the Creation narrative, we are told that "God saw the earth," but instead of the breathtaking beauty of the beginning, "here: it had gone to ruin (Fox)."[18]

Other creation stories also contain a tragic dimension. Hinduism imagines creation falling more and more into fear and illusion. Medieval Jewish mysticism believed that the "original vessels" of creation were too weak for the divine splendor, and broke apart. But the biblical story itself is unique in speaking about the consequences of this for the divine Love itself. As the Creator-Parent of the human race, God is "grieved to his heart," utterly "pained," and rues the day humanity was ever created.[19] Humanity as "the image of God" surely seems some cruel joke. Early on in the story, divine Love hits bottom. What will God do? Discard the humanity project the way a potter throws a misshapen, still-wet pot back into the primordial clay from which it sprang? Or continue to work with it? Courage is the capacity to move ahead in spite of despair.

Such despair can even hinder the desire to parent. Back in the turmoil of the late 1960s, a friend I'll call Grant was hesitant about committing procreation. His experiences in Vietnam, distress over environmental problems, and worries about the human future made him wonder if it was "fair" to bring a child into the world. We debated the issue long and hard before he and his wife conceived their first child.

As children are born, parents may also wish to have children in their "own image and likeness," but the kids are likely to have plans of their own that no amount of parental pressure or pleading can control. On the best days the surprises are about good developments. Yet even these may require an adjustment of expectations. The father who dreams of a football star son may be faced instead with the sinewy muscles of a burgeoning ballet dancer, or the feminist mother with a neo-conservative daughter.

Worst-case scenarios are tragic in the extreme. I once knew a couple whose son was arrested, tried, found guilty, and imprisoned for armed burglary in their very own small rural town. Everyone who knew them well said they were kind and caring people who had tried to raise their boy right. Now they hid behind closed doors in grief and shame.

Just so, God is portrayed as being "grieved to his heart." Like a parent yelling, "I could kill you," out of frustrated love and fear, at a child who has wrecked the family car and almost killed herself, the story portrays God pondering the destruction of the whole human race. But as the Story unfolds, God's fury is penetrated by mercy when, in one last glance, Noah "found favor," and the Father-Shepherd decides to risk yet once again.[20] Like a woman who has had repeated miscarriages yet tries once more to conceive, God courageously chooses parenthood once more, knowing now just how high the risk may be. Even Noah and his descendants run amok, but God persists, choosing the family of Abraham for special tutelage, risking failure again and again to see this perilous humanity project to a successful outcome. The depths of all parental resilience are rooted in a courage that continues to invest in life in spite of surprises, difficulties, and disappointments, all because its love of that life is too great to give up.

the courage to love

Parents are not the only people for whom love takes courage. Romantic lovers know this. The hesitation of one or both of the lovers to approach the other is a staple of romantic comedy, as are the rebuffs, difficulties, and misunderstandings that may beset the lovers as they wend their way toward mutual commitment. Being smitten by love takes no courage at all. But if one desires to pursue it, then one must summon the courage to approach the beloved. The Lover, in precisely this romantic sense, is one of the major biblical metaphors for God. Such love is known in every time and place, though only the modern West has elevated it to the major reason for marriage. The Rabbis chose to place, right in the midst of Scripture, a book of intensely romantic, highly erotic love poems to which they gave the exalted name *The Song of Songs*. At the ordinary level these are songs probably composed for weddings and possibly even to liven up funeral banquets![21] But the Rabbis, and the Church Fathers after them, saw this kind of love as a reflection in human life of God's love for humanity. This is *eros*, the raw, urgent, passionate desire of lover for beloved—not *agape*, the moral willingness to help a person in need or be kind to a stranger. According to the Song, such love is "strong as death and fierce as the grave," its raging flame flashing like fire.[22]

Not only at the beginning, but throughout the relationship lovers face the possibility of disappointment and betrayal. The vulnerable gesture of love may be unintentionally batted away, or the well-chosen gift may be unsuitable. But in this strong love, people can turn and embrace one another even when love has led them to encounters with each other that seem as "terrible as an army with banners."[23] The language may seem a bit purple, but anyone who has been married for many years can probably identify with the description. Relationships are sustained by the courage to reach out again, forgive once more, seek clarity in the midst of confusion, and change expectations more than once.

Courage beyond all reasonable calculation is sometimes needed to sustain relationships. More than one long-term marriage has survived the apparent "death" of the relationship. As a marriage counselor friend tells me, the "original contract" a couple makes, often unconsciously, seldom works for all the years of a relationship. Infatuation wanes, sexual passion settles down, people grow in new ways, or they discover that their fond dreams of a spouse changing to suit their own unrealistic dreams don't pan out. That "first love" can die, leaving people bereft. Sometimes lovers challenge each other to changes they do not wish to face.

One of the most tragic divorces I know happened to a couple married over twenty years. Right on schedule, the looming prospect of the empty nest forced them to face being more fully together. While both had complaints, the wife had long harbored career dreams she felt the husband blocked out of a fear of her becoming more independent. Such long-standing issues led to more conflict and intensive marriage counseling. One day, the husband announced he was willing to make some changes to support the wife in her career dreams, including moving if she found a desirable position. Just a few weeks later, to his astonishment, she announced that the marriage was over and she was leaving. Perhaps something in her could not face stepping out in courage to realize her long-harbored dreams. Perhaps she was unable to face the drastically altered dynamics of their relationship. For whatever reason, she wanted an escape, and took it.

Only courage can bring people to reexamine their expectations, see their partner in a new, more realistic light, and explore new possibilities—or "renegotiate the contract" as my friend puts it.

The relationship between God and humanity is presented in Scripture as just such a marital work-in-progress. In spite of repeated disappointments that provoke wrath, indignation, accusation, even threats about a "bill of divorce,"[24] the relationship is renewed again and again. God suffers because of humanity's betrayal, but cannot imagine declaring the beloved species a failure. "How can I give you up?" the prophet Hosea hears God say. "Therefore, I will now allure her, and bring her into the wilderness, and speak tenderly to her. . . .There she shall respond as in the days of her youth."[25]

the courage for justice-making

The divine Love not only struggles to win back the beloved, but is pictured as entering into the heart of the human battle against all that spoils the beloved's life: God's love enters into the struggle for justice. God dreams of a world filled with communities where people will "do justice, love kindness and walk humbly" according to the prophet Micah.[26] The biblical writers who have caught this dream see a God who struggles for us, with us, and through us to overturn injustices such as the Hebrew enslavement in Egypt, the oppression of the poor by the rich, and the outcasts by the established. "The Lord is a warrior," dedicated to justice, in this uphill battle against powerfully entrenched oppression.[27]

Most of the Psalms are the songs of people crying for such justice as they face cruel persecutors, mighty oppressors, and heartless enemies. As Psalm 10 describes them, they are the poor, marginal, or defeated for whom the wicked "lurk in secret like a lion in its covert" stealthily watching, that they may "murder the innocent."[28] Written from the underbelly of history, they chronicle the sorrows of those who, age after age, live in the thrall of tyranny and the oppression of exploitative leaders. "Rouse yourself," is the cry; "come to my help and see! . . . Take hold of shield and buckler . . . ! Draw the spear and javelin."[29]

God is portrayed constantly warring, not against "flesh and blood," as Paul tells us, but against all the spiritual "principalities and powers" such as greed, envy, and arrogance that enslave the human mind and drive the power of oppression in history.[30] This story of God's courageous fight for human good comes to a crescendo in the portrayal of Christ, in whom God's own qualities are "manifest in the flesh," as an early Christian hymn puts it.[31]

In one of the earliest interpretations of the meaning of the Cross, Christ is seen wading into the heart of our dilemma like a warrior coming to rescue the prisoners.[32] He must face in himself all the same fears, pains, sorrows, and difficulties as our own, yet he finds a way valiantly through them, opening that way to us.

Jesus is depleted at times by the work of healing, distressed by Israel's apparent failure to receive the glad tidings he brings, and "sorrowful unto death" at betrayal by his disciples. Trembling with acute fear in prayerful anguish before his arrest, he begs to be shown another way to accomplish his mission. Yet, when the enemy approaches, he rises to face the great trial of an unjust court and painful death not only with courage but with compassion for his enemies, who "do not know what they are doing."[33]

As he mounts the cross, what seems to onlookers an ignominious defeat is, inwardly, a victory deep within the soul of Christ and for the soul of humankind. The power of the "midnight sky" of God's vast love in his heart, this crucified man is really *Christus Victor,* the Braveheart who faces down the dark enemies of the human heart, entering into the core of our fear of abandonment to "spoil the spoiler of his prey"[34] by rescuing us from the dark Tempter who would enslave us to our own fears, resentments, and resistance. His way of suffering opens the prison of the heart to bring light, healing, and release to all "held in slavery by the fear of death."[35] The living and dying of Jesus Christ is God's startling revelation of the love that comes among us, willing to suffer whatever battle scars are necessary to release us from whatever prison we have wandered into.

This is a Love that unmasks, challenges, and disarms the causes of suffering. Francis of Assisi was inspired by it to abandon the security of his cozy merchant-class home and lucrative prospects to challenge the hard-heartedness of his own economic class by living in solidarity with the poor. By its power Martin Luther King, Jr., taught nonviolent resistance as a way to undermine brutal discrimination. It guides the patient counselor's listening heart as she wrestles in spiritual warfare to bring the hiding, fearful aspects of the human psyche into the light of a larger, saner world, and hearts are freed to claim life more fully. All these people participate in some share of the Love that walks through darkest hell to burst the bonds of fear and death.

This is why Christ can teach us how to face opposition and difficulty in a way that releases us from the narrowness of spirit and shrinkage of soul that suffering can so easily foster. God is undeterred by anything human history and the wildness of nature can imagine. Paul assures us, in his great vision of cosmic suffering in Romans 8, that nothing can separate us from a love so deep, broad, and high that it can share our suffering and not be undone by it.[36] God is more than willing to give us a share in the courageous Love that invites us to stay rooted, in our darkest hours, in the Goodness that gives birth to our own courage to create, parent, love, and struggle for what we cherish as holy, just, and good.

no good answer: beyond the reasons

"WHY?" IS ALMOST ALWAYS THE FIRST question that arises when suffering strikes. The mind reels and searches for a reason, whether there is a good one or not.

Donna's baffled grief over the murder of her husband was sharpened by the growth of their first child, *his* first child, within her. She and Jeff had come from small towns in the South to the slums of New York City on a great spiritual adventure, joining other twenty-somethings in a ministry to educate, evangelize, and empower inner-city kids. They lived right there in the neighborhood, sharing the life of those with whom they worked. Now the neighborhood's random violence had claimed Jeff's life.

"Why him?" she screamed. "Why now, just as we are beginning a family? How could God let this happen when we followed his call to come to this dangerous neighborhood to love and serve him?" Not only the head but the heart cries out for as many reasons for such a tragedy as possible. A counselor friend says people cope better with adversity if they find "a framework of meaning" rather than feeling tossed about helplessly in a swirl of senselessness.

But no matter how loudly she cried, Donna got no comforting answer, at least not one that comforted her. Just because we ask "Why?" doesn't mean we will discover a really satisfying "because." There may be reasonable explanations for some forms of suffering, some from science, some from religion, some from just plain common sense, but they don't necessarily add up to an explanation for why life is the way it is, so full of the possibility of sorrow. A host of "little becauses" like these doesn't add up to the Big Answer human beings feel they need in the face of suffering.

the little "becauses" are seldom enough

There was one clearly identifiable reason for Jeff's death. The most immediate cause for Jeff's death was that he and Donna lived in a violent neighborhood where street crime was commonplace. The attack, so far as any one could tell, wasn't motivated by personal hostility, or resentment of the group's religious work. A senseless act of rage, perhaps by a frustrated mugger, had felled the young idealist. This enthusiastic band of urban missioners now saw more clearly the nature of the community they had chosen to serve.

But why such random violence? They already knew some of the "little" answers to that question: joblessness and poverty, the terrible state of the schools, and the hopeless sense of abandonment created by the flight of business and the neglect of government. Some found the strength to cope in these circumstances. But for others family life often unraveled, drug and alcohol abuse abounded, petty crime offered the chance to eke out a living, and gangs cultivated a culture of macho swagger and easy violence. Worse yet, some people respond to adversity by going down the path of bitterness, resentment, and a desire to strike back at something, anything, in revenge for their plight—even those who have come to help.

All these "little reasons" fall short of a comprehensive reason for Jeff's death, at least for people who believe in a just and good God. Such explanations offer cold comfort for a sorrow like Donna's. This doesn't mean that we should neglect them just because they don't add up to an ultimate Big Answer. The Bible's catalog of "little becauses" for specific suffering is sane and sensible: ignorance, destructive sinfulness, and the wildness of the world.

some suffering is caused by ignorance

Our ignorance may come from lack of information about how the human spirit functions best. While we do not, as some popular New Age teachers claim, "create our own reality," how we respond to situations affects the very shape of the self, and sometimes the outcome of events. As spiritual teachings from all over the world and modern psychology show us, unrealistic expectations, resistance to change, refusal to accept facts, or a grudging chronic pessimism can make real suffering worse, or actually create suffering in situations where we face only a challenge.

The ignorance may be about the world itself. Ignorant nutrition may lead to disease, as it did for those who suffered from pellagra because we didn't know the importance of vitamin B. Ignorance about DDT caused the near-extinction of the bald eagle. Continuing ignorance about the long-term effect of pesticides, household toxins, plastics, and humanly generated electromagnetism may be contributing to various forms of cancer and autoimmune disorder.

Ignorance may come from inexperience. The old and wise voice of "your father's instruction and . . . your mother's teaching" in the opening chapter of *Proverbs* goes to great pains to warn the ignorant young man against joining gangs that promise "all kinds of costly things" through lying in ambush to rob. Such behavior sets "an ambush," yes, but it is "for their own lives."[37] Learn from the voice of experience, and save your life.

Sometimes we flee one danger only to run ignorantly into the jaws of another. Most researchers now agree that our antibiotic war against bacteria is producing "super-bugs"—new strains of venereal disease, tuberculosis, and streptococcus—for which there are few if any remedies. Even on a family level, the attempt to make one's house "germ-free" may be contributing to the rise of asthma in children whose immature immune systems haven't been challenged to develop by encountering enough bacteria. To those trapped by such ignorance the world can seem like the prophet Amos's nightmarish vision of the man who "fled from a lion, and was met by a bear."[38]

The Scriptures are also clear about the only remedy—increased knowledge: "The beginning of wisdom is this: Get wisdom, and whatever else you get, get insight."[39] Biblical religion is solidly on the side of the scientific impulse to dispel our ignorance of how the world works, as well as supportive of increasing the skills that enable us to avoid unnecessary suffering.

some suffering is caused by destructive behavior.

Smoking cigarettes can kill you. Everybody knows that, even tobacco companies. We called them "cancer-sticks" when I was a kid, long before the Surgeon General's report in the late 1960s and the appearance of warning labels on cigarette packages. Neither that, nor my mother's hacking smoker's cough, nor the fundamentalist preachers' wise warnings that smoking desecrates our bodies, the "temple of the Holy Spirit," kept me from chain-smoking for seventeen years.

Call it an addiction, if you like, for that is one reason it was so difficult to stop. Bring the tobacco companies to trial for their conspiracy to suppress evidence, for they are surely culpable. Sue the movie companies and advertisers for making smoking so alluring that it enticed a fundamentalist boy with inclinations toward sophistication and worldliness, for they did. But the stark truth is that I wasn't ignorant: I made a choice in the face of dire warnings and clear knowledge that this was both a sin against my body and a risk to my health. My smoking could have led to disaster. Both my parents died of smoking-related emphysema. So far it looks like I stopped soon enough, in my late thirties, for the damage to repair itself. But if I had developed emphysema, could I really ask God why?

Sin, as the Bible understands it, is not some breaking of arbitrary rules set down by a tyrannical God to control humanity, but destructive action against ourselves or others that undermines God's desire for our good. Even Jesus the healer seems to link some (though not all) sicknesses with sin, as when he says to the paralytic, "Your sins are forgiven," as a prelude to the man's release from paralysis.[40] His own guilt may have led to hysterical paralysis.

This is as true of corporate sins as of personal ones. If we build our city on the flood plain, we need not blame God for the flood damage. If the privileged oppress the poor long enough, they will reap increased crime and violence. Sections of Sicily, once the breadbasket of ancient Rome, face possible desertification today because most of Sicily's forests were cut down in the eighteenth and nineteenth centuries for charcoal and other commercial purposes. This was not simple ignorance, but defiance of the common good. In the face of a global warming trend exacerbated by humanity's dependence on fossil fuels, the race between impending desert and reforestation is on. If farmers and loggers cut down all the trees, less rain will fall. If the melting of the Greenland ice cap due to global warming causes oceans to rise, the threat to coastal cities and vacation islands will not be God's doing.

Biblical people would have seen the rising oceans as "the wrath of God." Such language is not about some petty vindictiveness on God's part, but rather the consequence of going against the grain of creation. As we saw in Chapter Two, "wrath" is "anthropathic" language for being dead set against something. Both the fabric of nature and the moral commandments are God's way of wisdom for earth and its creatures, loving guidance for sensible living in a difficult world. There's "hell to pay," as we put it in popular speech, if you go down certain paths, simply because they are intrinsically hellish. The cure is not magical rites, bloody sacrifices, or paroxysms of guilt, but change of behavior.

some suffering is from the world's wildness

Much suffering, however, seems simply arbitrary. The sins of the Sicilian nobility may have cut down the forests, but did not cause the devastating earthquake that killed hundreds of thousands of Sicilians in 1693. The tens of thousands made homeless by tornadoes or hurricanes each year do not deserve these catastrophes. As freak weather (rather than mechanical failure) precipitates a plane crash, the talented young artist on board, the group of teens on their way home from a European singing tour, or the secretary who just survived breast cancer have done nothing to invite their deaths. Such events are part of the strange level of "frustration" or "futility" in this world that Paul alludes to in his vision of cosmic suffering.[41]

This world of awesome beauty, exquisite order, and abundant goodness also pulses with chaotic forces like weather and bacterial infection that have a wild and dangerous edge. The human race is subject to stormy outbreaks of war that seem to fly in the face of all common sense. Why?

For those who believe there is no reality but nature itself, the answer is simple enough: The universe is the way it is because that is the way it is. But for any who believe this world sprang into being from a good and loving Source, the harshness of its contours, the danger of its freedoms, and the magnitude of its suffering pose a great challenge.

It comes as a surprise to discover that the Bible has no comprehensive Big Answer to this question, no ultimate reason for the mystery of such arbitrary suffering. There are no footnotes explaining why the serpent is in the garden, no comprehensive explanation as to why the weather system faces us with tempest, fire, and flood. There are no direct, declarative statements about why humans have been given free will or allowed to have ever-increasing godlike capacities to do good or evil. There is not even any clear and definitive reason given for why the universe was created at all, or why it is loaded with so much potential suffering. The fabric of reality is as it is, not some other way, as is the reality of God. There is no biblical story that justifies the popular impression that the nature of the universe is the way it is because God chose this universe out of a number of other possibilities. Scripture is interested in the possibilities of human life in *this* universe rather than speculating about any alternative one. Why this is a universe of creatures exquisitely attuned to both pleasure and pain—and therefore prone to suffer—remains an enigma not puzzled out by Scripture.

There are some clues, to be sure. Scripture declares that the foundation and structure of creation are good, and that God's aim for creatures—"bringing many children to glory," as the author of *Hebrews* puts it—is even better.[42] But as we have seen, the wild, chaotic freedom of its origins remains part of the world's ongoing structure. This freedom is an inviolable part of the fabric of nature, as it flows naturally from the divine nature itself.

The natural forces themselves follow their own nature without regard for human vulnerabilities. Hurricanes do not "punish" the Florida coast, as the newscasters trumpet, but simply blow. Human beings are left free to make mistakes. Jeff was not gunned down on that South Bronx street because of some personal sin he had committed, but because of the reckless exercise of the killer's freedom. It is more accurate to say that such freely chosen murder could not be stopped than that God could not stop it, because such is the fabric of reality once creation is set in motion.[43] The difficulty of living in this kind of world is at the heart of Donna's wondering tears about her husband's murder.

Unwilling to live with biblical enigma, theologians have tried to construct an ultimate Big Answer: All catastrophe, from earthquakes to erosion, must be the result of Adam's sin; the Devil is the source of everything bad in the world; every difficulty is a test to see if we're faithful; it's all a sometimes painful but truly necessary educational experience. Eastern philosophies, based on worldviews different from those of the biblical world, tend to take the educational approach: We're on the karmic wheel of existence until we wake up and realize the self-inflicted causes of our suffering. Then we can achieve release. While there may be some partial truth in each of these theological mega-answers, none, finally, seems an adequate Big Answer.

God's unexpected answer

But is a Big Answer what we really want or basically need? In the book of *Job*, the Bible's great epic poem about suffering, it becomes clear that we live in a truly enigmatic universe—one in which a loving God and terrible suffering are simply co-present. Job, the Bible's archetypal innocent sufferer, is not satisfied by all the "little becauses" his friends offer to convince him that his suffering has come for good reasons. No, Job protests, he has done nothing to deserve this. If this is a test of faith, it is beyond all reason. And no, he will not bow before the mystery of such unjust treatment. He'll cry until he gets an answer. In the end, God agrees with Job that all the friends' "little reasons" were wrong, and gives Job a different kind of gift.

God's answer to Job comes, not as a philosophy of suffering, but as a manifestation of Presence, a revelation of divine splendor shining through the beauty *and* terror of a tempestuous universe. No explanations are given, but rather a call for Job to "stand up" in the midst of life's whirlwind. From Job's standpoint, the reasons for the suffering remain an enigma. Job's wholly unexpected answer is an encounter with the Divine: "I had heard of you by the hearing of the ear, but now my eye sees you."[44] In the face of this, his old ways of seeing the universe are "undone," and he is able to recreate his life in a new light.[45]

Donna didn't get an answer, either, but a Presence. One night as she poured out her sadness and confusion in prayer, "It was as if something gentle came over me and literally pulled the painful, physical misery of my grief out of me. I was then filled with a quiet, soothing calmness. I knew that somehow, I knew not how, it would be ok, I would be ok." As she continued to pray, this reassuring calmness took the form of a waking dream: "I was going through a dark tunnel, like the 'spooky' tunnels in the Fun House at the amusement park. I knew that off there in the dark there were all kinds of scary forces. Then I realized that the 'boat' in which I traveled wasn't a boat at all, but a huge hand, God's hand. I was given to understand that no matter how big the troubles I might face were, God's hand was bigger still. Deep down underneath all my concerns and worries, there was no reason for me to be afraid."

Donna, like Job, had been answered by a Presence, not a reason. As Moses was told when God sent him to face hardship in Egypt:

"I will be with you."[46] Christ is the ultimate sign of "Emmanuel," God-with-us in the difficulties of the world. This is the Bible's only ultimate answer to the mystery of suffering, deserved or undeserved, in this world. Sharing our life, God seeks to bring good out of anything that happens to us, no matter how small or great the difficulty may be, weaving a web of grace even in senseless events. That presence, accepted by us, can give firm ground for our halting courage, alert us inwardly to opportunities, and work through our prayer and reflection to guide us, and Donna's framework of meaning became that promise of presence.

I've had some tastes of that Presence in my own difficulties, but one of the most poignant moments was while enduring an unanticipated onslaught of anxiety and dread as I slowly emerged from my prison cell of buried emotional pain. So unfamiliar were these feelings, welling up from hidden depths, that I felt disoriented. The practice of spiritual disciplines that might have sustained me unraveled: Contemplative prayer withered, daily t'ai chi flagged, and the only refuge left seemed to be burying myself in fiction, an old escape. Worse yet, part of me harbored resentment that God was treating me this way. Just a few weeks before, I had opened myself for healing, and part of me now felt betrayed, just as the Hebrew slaves resented the God who began their liberation by rousing Pharaoh's tyranny to full flower. I felt, as St. Teresa of Avila is reported to have quipped when her ox cart overturned, "If this is the way you treat all your friends, it's little wonder you have so few of them."

The divine mercy was, of course, not intimidated by my resentment. One morning, the book I picked up literally fell open to a passage about the surge of suppressed dark emotions that the practice of contemplative prayer can sometimes release as God's grace slowly works its way into all the crevices of our woundedness. When I came downstairs to put the morning coffee on, sparkling dew in the summer sunrise drew me out into the beauty of the dawning day. In a rare moment, my inner resentment dissolved, and I opened myself to the Source of this beauty. Immediately I felt surrounded, supported, and profoundly understood. Without condemnation or judgment, it was made crystal clear to me that I could be doing a lot better at self-care than I was. But even as I failed at that, this Love knew better than I did what I was going through. In that moment, the silent communication was more than enough to reassure me that all was, fundamentally, well. I fed on that food in the wilderness for weeks to come, as the dread diminished, leaving me healed of its dark power, able to face life with less fear than ever before.

divine love and human suffering—mysteriously co-present

This strange appearance of a sense of divine compassion co-present with hardship and pain is as much a perennial fact of human experience as suffering itself. We may not be able, logically, to reconcile these opposites in a grand mega-theory of the universe, but we are faced with the widespread persistence of such experiences. Why should we reject these signs of divine love simply because we can't figure out exactly how they square with a world of enigmatic suffering? The Scriptures do not fear to let the enigma of life in its mingled suffering and joy stand. This is the way life on this planet is, and God is involved in it all the way to the hard wood of the cross, courageously sharing the narrow spaces of our suffering and shouldering the burden of it with us, fully present, working with us, in us, through us to open it up to the larger reality of grace.

As my friend Tilly-Jo discovered it when she was praying for John, a beloved priest dying of cancer, "I came to feel as if there are two levels of reality: a spacious one where everything somehow fits together in a pattern which is suffused with astounding love and understanding, and another, narrow, cramped level where everything seems rough, confusing, and disordered. Sometimes the two come together when I pray, and I'm present to John's suffering, my sorrow over it, and the sense of helplessness we all feel, and simultaneously I know that, deep down, everything is OK and John's disease is somehow being folded into God's loving purposes for him now and beyond death."

The Scriptures say the same thing in a slightly different way: "God works together with those who love him to bring about what is good," or the more familiar "in all things God works for the good."[47] No matter what happens, or whatever its immediate cause, the crux of the matter is how we let the Spirit work through us to align our response to God's most creative possibilities for the situation. Nothing is outside of God's ability to redeem and fit into a pattern for good.

This co-presence of suffering and compassion is one aspect of the framework of meaning revealed not only in human experience, but in the overall story told by Scripture. Such a framework of meaning that can help us be open to love and see the possibility of new life even in the most tragic circumstances is gospel—"good news"—indeed. Such experiences invite us to trust this unconquerable love and let it strengthen our resilience as we face confusion, frustration, and even seeming futility.

heart prayer

O Heart of my heart,
O Mind of my mind,
Deep Breath of my little breathing,
Great Life of my little living,
Great Love of my little loving,
Be Thou to me all that is:
Be Thou to me everything that moves me to shine,
All things that craft me supple and caring,
All souls and creatures that root me in love.
Be Thou also to me companion in every adversity,
Blessing them to be the challenges
that provoke me to deeper resources of soul,
that grow me deep and strong
however weak I may seem to be.
Be Thou to me my truest life,
My All in all,
Thou Heart
and Mind
and
Breath of my being!

PART TWO

skillful means
for suffering redemptively

CHAPTER FOUR
reweaving the fabric of meaning

A FRAMEWORK OF MEANING is necessary
for feeling our lives make sense. Intense suffering like that which
Donna or Job encountered creates a rupture in the fabric of personal
meaning, causing profound and life-threatening disorientation.
Meaning is, almost literally, food for our souls, necessary for survival.
We know this, because people can fall ill and die without it.

It is a well-known fact that the surviving spouse of a long-term
marriage is more vulnerable to disease and even death in the year after
losing a partner. Life just doesn't have the same meaning anymore.

More than one professional has fallen emotionally or physically
ill soon after retiring from a well-loved career. Depression is not
uncommon, and the highest suicide rate is found among white
men over sixty-five. Probable cause? Loss of meaning. "Doing
nothing can take its toll," says Abigail Trafford in *The Washington
Post.* "With the loss of work, there's a loss of personhood. How do
you find purpose in work and meaning in relationship in these
decades?"[48]

Ancient peoples called this malaise "soul-loss." We hear the
ancient Israelite exiles in Babylon make just such a cry of from the
heart in Psalm 137:

> *By the rivers of Babylon, there we sat down,*
> *yea, we wept, when we remembered Zion. . . .*
> *How shall we sing the LORD'S song in a strange land?*[49]

Or to state it in plain modern English: *Who am I now that this has happened? What kind of a world is this, anyway? What purpose do I have in this strange land?*

Sociologists have noted modern occurrences of soul-loss in African tribes relocated from their ancestral lands, and migrants from the country now living in the crowded cities, cut off from tribal relationships, communal practices, and ancient symbols. The most famous case was a tribe relocated in the 1950s which lost all of its former social graces. A people who had lived by an ethic of mutual help became almost universally mean-spirited and stingy. Life had become meaningless.

Adversity can catapult us into just such a dangerous "strange land," where the familiar landmarks of meaning are blurred or destroyed. Donna's anguished "why" about the murder of her husband, the sense of disorientation in depressed professionals, the typical murmurs of "incredible" and "incomprehensible" about great natural disasters, or the vague dis-ease of people whose work or relationships are somehow not suited to their real selves, all witness to the power of feeling bereft of the familiar, life-sustaining ingredients of meaning.

What are these life-giving ingredients? Meaning is a complex phenomenon, but my observations of its loss and recovery as a pastor over many years have led me to believe that meaning includes at least three factors: a sense of *mattering,* a sense of *felt relationship to things good and valuable,* and a sense of *living within a story* that relates us, consciously or unconsciously, to a purposeful reality.

we need to feel we matter

"What does it matter?" laments the recently bereaved widower about any encouragement to "get involved," and then goes on, "What do I matter?" At the most intense, the loss of a loved one can lead to a feeling, however temporary, that nothing matters. We find a sense of usefulness in caring for a spouse, raising a child, or relating to a beloved job that gives life purposeful meaning. More essentially, we know that what we do is important to the loved one or enterprise. This gives us a sense of location in a known world of relationships, of significance so subtle we seldom realize its importance until it is lost. Losing a job, moving to a new location, getting divorced, or even getting promoted to greater responsibility at work can cause disorientation, and a crisis of meaning, however minor.

As a third grader, I had a streak of social timidity that flared occasionally. When faced with promotion to the intermediate Sunday School from my familiar elementary department, I became a Sunday School drop-out rather than face the disruption in my secure world. Who would I be in this strange new land? I still remember Mrs. Draper, our beloved first- through third-grade teacher, marching us all down the hall to the bigger, more populous intermediate room to see where we'd go in the fall and to introduce us to the new teacher. As I cased the room, looking up at the taller kids, my timidity simply decided it wasn't going to let me take it there. What would this new world be like? To whom would I matter?

Out of this experience I have great sympathy for all the "displaced" suburban children I've had in Sunday School over the years, new to the community, some of them really feeling lost and alone from the inevitable dislocation. They don't know what they mean any more. Such human response to dislocation underlines why a sense of mattering to God provides for so many an important thread of meaning in the midst of change. The Jewish people survived the exile in Babylon primarily because they held fast to their relationship to the God they struggled to understand in their new circumstances.

It may seem surprising, even intellectually dissatisfying, for all of Job's pressing philosophical questions to dissolve in his encounter with the presence of God, but this kind of deliverance from a meaning crisis does happen in real life.

An old college buddy phoned some years back in the throes of an upheaval both marital and spiritual. Long unhappy in a marriage originally precipitated by premarital pregnancy, the man I'll call Louis had fallen into a passionate, clandestine love affair with a neighbor, a woman similarly miserable in her marriage. Both of them were pious fundamentalist Christians, guilt-torn by their behavior, but carried away nonetheless by their desirous need for each other. For my friend, this affair was not only a moral dislocation, but the eruption of an equally passionate spiritual quest. The tight world of his fundamentalist background had been torn open by need, confusion, and questioning. By turns confused and depressed, excited and overjoyed, he searched for new meaning: He read depth psychology, wondered about psychic phenomena, dived into literary criticism of the Bible, and talked my head off on the phone at least once a month for half a year.

And then, suddenly, all the urgency went out of the quest. Louis and his lover faced the brokenness of their marriages. Regretful as they were over their actions, divorce seemed the only possible course for them, for they believed their marriages had long since died. They went through that painful process, and then married each other. As soon as the decision was made to do this, the yawning gates that had opened onto cosmic confusion closed, and Louis's life was ordered once again with new meaning and purpose.

My purpose is neither to applaud nor condemn Louis, but simply to note how the assurance of a loving presence in a new marriage stilled his burning cosmic questions. My friend now knew for sure that he mattered to someone he loved. The world made sense again. The power of knowing we're not alone in facing the difficulties of life is a major factor in making suffering bearable, and giving us a sense that we can face painful challenges redemptively.

we need relationship to things good and valuable

Simply feeling related to something good is one of the most powerful ingredients in creating a sense of meaning I know. It can also, like mattering to someone, quite mysteriously dissolve the confusion of meaninglessness, or at least soften its intensity.

During a bleak period in her life, a friend I'll call Ellen had pulled her leaden body out of bed and trudged off to work wondering if there was any reason to live. As her spirits seemed to reach their nadir, her eye was caught by a glint of sunlight shining through a drop of water on a leaf near the office door. This drop of liquid light invited her to turn, behold, and marvel. In her misery she could have easily shrugged off the invitation. Instead, she stopped and took in the delicate colors. As she did so, all her feelings seemed to rearrange themselves around this beauty at the center of her awareness. "In the space of a moment, life seemed bearable again," she told me, "offering possibilities of simple joys like this I had forgotten in my gloom. All those other feelings were still there; but somehow they didn't seem so overwhelming. I was being given a chance to choose what I would feed on in the hours to come—my misery or this miracle. All day long that drop of sunlight kept capturing the center of my heart."

Ellen was delivered from suicidal feelings through her encounter with the rainbow droplet of light. Suddenly life was worth living again. Her innate framework of meaning had been reactivated by the simple experience of something full of goodness. The raindrop brought back to life a whole world of good associations, the tapestry of values that gave meaning to her life.

But it's not only experiencing goodness that can create a sense of meaning. So can *doing* good. Victims of major tragedy cope better if they can "find something worthwhile to do," according to my friend Dr. Robert Clark, a family therapist and lecturer in Medical Humanities at Drew University. Clark knows this from bitter personal experience. His own daughter was "mowed down by a drug-crazed driver who aimed right at my two daughters and their cousin." The man, as it turned out, "was a sociopath," according to Dr. Clark, who has wrestled both personally and professionally with the desire to do vengeance that such crimes provoke. The ache of wanting to "rip the offender apart limb from limb"—and being unable to—is part of the suffering. As a good therapist, Bob knows these feelings must be faced frankly and openly, or they can destroy the survivors, both individually and as a family unit. Divorce, for example, is not an uncommon aftereffect of a tragedy befalling a child.

Since vengeance is a "do something" response, albeit destructive, Clark feels the survivors must channel that energy into doing something constructive. Such a crisis forces you "to decide what your values are," because they are the "building blocks for a framework of meaning in which the tragedy can make some sense—even if the only sense is doing something good in response to it."

He and his wife decided almost immediately to donate his daughter's organs to a donor bank. The urgency to do something good was intensified when they discovered "how little the life of a child is worth in the eyes of the law." The couple then campaigned to change the New Jersey penalty for slaughter by auto. Though their effort made little dent in the law, Bob feels it was worthwhile. Part of his larger framework has been to work in personal therapy with families victimized by such events. Doing good helps mends the fabric of both soul and world.

When the world was appalled by the Christmastide 2004 tsunami disaster that killed over 150,000 along the shores of the Indian Ocean, a counter-wave of good deeds followed. Nations and individuals contributed millions of dollars. My neighbor, a highly skilled professional, e-mailed me, asking if I had direct contacts with relief organizations that might be able to use his experience in transportation and regional planning for the rebuilding efforts. Other friends circulated the addresses of relief agencies. Local villagers whose nearby inland communities had been spared, reached out to take in orphaned children and get them back in school immediately, reorienting them to something familiar.

We humans instinctively try to make meaning out of whatever seems overwhelmingly meaningless, by creating good, as if to re-balance the equilibrium of the world. If the forces of nature seem to treat human life with such disregard for its significance, human beings push back by creating significance in the face of implacable forces. Our species cannot live in a meaningless world.

This urgent need in human nature for meaning is, surely, one of the signs that the universe is not devoid of ultimate meaning and purpose. Even to a pure naturalist, it must seem exceedingly odd that a supposedly "accidental" universe has evolved a creature so hungry for meaning.

we need to live within a story

For Christian faith, of course, this universe is no accident, but is part of the larger framework of God's creative and redemptive love, a story told from Genesis to Revelation. Large frameworks of meaning usually take story form, as in the stories that portray God's different roles in Scripture as discussed in Chapter Two.

Story can touch us so deeply because it is the fundamental way our brains organize information, according to Dr. Daniel Dunnett, one of the world's leading brain researchers. Even so great a skeptic as Dunnet, who sees the brain as a computer and the sense of self as a highly functional delusion, is impressed with the brain's "innate storytelling program."[50] Even the simplest sentence is a mini-narrative, with a subject, verb, and object; from "the dog chased the cat" to "God so loved the world," it's almost impossible not to see the world in story form.

Even an object is a set of stories finished and potential. As a teenager in one of my discussion groups once put it, "A noun is just a verb that has slowed down for a while."[51] The world is story. So is every person. Contrary to much modern assumption, there's no such thing as a "fact" without an implied framework of meaning.[52] Little surprise, then, that story is such a crucial ingredient in human meaning, for it is the main way we have of "framing" facts with meanings.

Story can appear in minimalist form: "That's the way the cookie crumbles" or "whoever has the most toys when he dies wins" both imply whole philosophies of life. Even to say, as do many scientists, that the universe is a "glorious accident" is the beginning of a story, which they then narrate in great detail, from the initial cosmic fireball to our present state of development.

People who believe there is no underlying meaning in the universe still find inspiration in that story of cosmic development. Against its background brave modern existentialists and humanists like Franz Kafka tell their stories of how humans create meaning in the face of what they believe is a purposeless and uncaring universe. We cannot survive without this framing of facts into meanings, as the post-World War II psychologist Viktor Frankl saw so clearly in his studies of concentration camp survivors. Those who survived had created a story, either of finding meaning through power and collaboration with the guards, or through helping others to survive.[53]

As in the camps, the threat of death forces the issue of meaning on us, and forces us to review the story of our life. While many do this without conscious deliberation, one man I know tackled the issue directly. The person I'll call Martin, a vigorous man in his early sixties, still had the trim build of the competition runner he had been in his twenties when the odd twinges and sudden weaknesses he had begun suffering were diagnosed as a degenerative disease for which there is no known cure, only the prospect of steady decline into physical immobility, with the unclouded mind trapped in helpless flesh.

As the initial shock began to wear off, Martin and his wife Anna were "plunged into a search for meaning." He had been a devout Christian in his youth, "altar boy and everything, but drifted away from it in adulthood." He had created a life where meaning was found in family, an interesting career, and good friends. That family-and-career story, as well as his own philosophical musings, true as they might be, were now too small to contain a disruption as great as this disease.

"We read everything we could get our hands on," Martin told me, "books and articles about the disease, of course, but also about the meaning of life. We watched the videotapes of Bill Moyers and Campbell discussing *The Power of Myth*. Maybe in these sacred stories we could find some sense of the meaning of life in the face of death."

I crossed Martin and Anna's path when one of their friends said he was interested in the spiritual sharing group she belonged to at my education center. Martin wished he could belong to one himself. By this time he was weak and used a walker. His speech was beginning to slur, so we decided to form a special group just for Martin at his home. We spent a number of evenings simply sharing our own feelings and beliefs about the most basic question he posed: "Now that I'm about to die, how does my life matter? What does it all mean in the face of death?" He was not interested in canned answers, especially assurances it would all be made better in an afterlife.

All the themes spelled out in this chapter wove their way into the conversation, sooner or later. As he told the story of his life, ways he had mattered, valuable activities and people all emerged. Only one specifically religious story surfaced, but it was a powerful one. One day, soon after his diagnosis, Martin had been alone and was startled to hear a voice within himself saying, clearly and compassionately, "You are not alone—I am with you."

One evening, as his condition worsened, he raised the very practical question: How could he decide when the quality of life had deteriorated so far that fighting to stay alive no longer made sense? He wasn't contemplating suicide, but rather how many extraordinary means—like the intravenous feeding he was already receiving—he should use to prolong life.

The group, which included some skilled psychologists, gave a variety of practical but highly conceptual responses. Martin nodded, considering each; but none seemed to touch him very deeply. Finally, I told a story that had been created many years earlier by another dying person I was companioning, a woman whose liver cancer had begun to undermine her ability to keep on living with any normalcy.

"Having this disease has been like waking up one day and discovering I'm lost in a jungle," the woman I'll call Kathryn had told me. "For a year now I've been trying to get back to the coastal city, to normal civilization, but now I'm wondering, not only if I'll make it back, but how long I should try to do so." I asked her, "Do you still want to keep trying?" Tearfully, she nodded "yes." "Well, what if we think of it this way?" I said. "Every day when you get up, you ask yourself if you feel you can keep on heading back to the city. If the answer is yes, get as far as you can, then rest. But some morning you may wake up, and you won't feel like going on.

What would you like to do if that happens?" Her answer was quick: "Find a nice tree and curl up under it."

The parable we had created satisfied her, and guided her last days, helping her to decide when to "curl up" for her dying in a beloved vacation home surrounded by family. As I told the story to Martin, it seemed to satisfy something in him as well. He took a deep breath, as if to drink it in, smiled slightly, nodded assent, and indicated that the evening discussion was over. The story conveyed a meaning deeper than abstractions, and provided a way to manage his expectations until the time he, too, decided it was time to "curl up," and as he put it, "go home."

sacred story has deep power

The jungle parable revealed itself to Kathryn's imagination in response to handling a specific life challenge. Martin reached out for even larger stories, as his investigations into mythology and sacred story indicate.

Only sacred story is large and deep enough to indicate human suffering can be redeemed and made ultimately meaningful. The largest form of story is the great sacred Saga or Myth, which tells how the gods, or the spiritual patterns of Ultimate Reality, or God are shaping all life toward divinely desired purposes. The smaller meanings of our lives find more coherent shape when they can be seen in the light of the larger meanings provided by sacred story.

By "myth" I mean a story so true that it happens again and again in different ways throughout history, rather than a tale historically untrue. It may or may not have actually happened at a point in human history. Stories like the attack on Pearl Harbor or the crucifixion of Jesus are about real historical events, but are mythic in dimension because these events reveal timelessly repeated patterns of deception, miscommunication, and betrayal, if you prefer. Myths like that of the beautiful Narcissus, on the other hand, who so fell in love with his own image reflected in the water that he drowned, never happened historically, but the pattern of drowning in self-preoccupation is relived tragically in thousands of lives. Good myths reveal deep truths about the perennial patterns of divine or human activity.

Total rationalists and secularists who do not use religious myths still use stories, often unconsciously, to stretch a "sacred canopy" of values, and will defend them with religious fervor.[54] The battle between creationists and evolutionists, for example, is not about scientific fact alone, but about the values inherent in the different stories. Did human life originate by purposive, "intelligent design" or random "natural selection"?

It matters what sacred story we choose to live in. As a Christian I believe that the great biblical saga of a good universe emerging from the heart of a good God, in which all challenges can be woven into a pattern for good, is the most profound story ever available for people facing difficulty and evil. The Gospel proclamation that grace can work through even the most death-dealing circumstance to bring new life can give a sense of purpose in the face of any suffering.

I realized how important that story is to me when a man told me about teaching the story of Easter to his children. The man I'll call Joshua, whose moral integrity I greatly admire, lives primarily by the scientific story of reality, raising his son and daughter to live in a "realistic" universe. Though neither a church-goer nor a believer himself, Joshua wants them to know their cultural Christian heritage, so he teaches them the stories of the great festivals as they occur. During a recent Easter season, as he told his seven-year-old son the story of Jesus' resurrection for the first time, the boy blurted out incredulously, "But, Daddy, people don't come to life again, do they? That's not possible." Joshua agreed.

At this point in the conversation, I surprised Joshua and myself by gasping audibly. Josh and I live in different universes because we live by different stories about life. I understand what Josh is trying to do, and applaud his wanting his children to know the sacred stories. I understand exactly why his scientifically schooled son responded the way he did. But, in that moment, I realized that *I have never lived in a universe where no one ever rose from the dead.*

For me the Easter story speaks about a real moment when resurrection actually happened in a real human life. Because of believing this story, I live in a world where Jesus Christ breaks the bonds of any kind of death, manifesting a pattern repeated over and over again in human lives.

Of course, Joshua had gone on to explain to his son that the Easter story is "a symbol for new life" like the renewal of the earth at the springtime, but for me the story is more than metaphor. My whole approach to life is dominated by the lively expectation that no matter what form death takes, it can be a doorway to resurrection—and that this power reaches even into the depths of physical death itself. The story's images have come to live inside me, guiding my expectations even when I hardly know it, making me look for the possibilities of resurrection in the darkest moments of my life.

My heart went out to this little boy who is being raised without the deep expectation that believing this story can engender. Yet so substantial is the reality of resurrection that I am confident it surrounds his life and is seeking to work in it, even though for now the Easter tale is mere legend to him. At least he knows the tale, and I pray that it will leap to life for him in some unforeseen future circumstance.

story can reframe difficult experiences

All the great biblical stories are filled with the power to frame our lives with meaning, and to reframe difficult experiences in the light of a larger reality. The "let my people go" story of Moses and the Exodus helped the African slaves in America reframe the sorrow of their experience into hope for the future. The story of Jesus' nonviolent response to evil inspired the world-shaking work of Ghandi and a host of those who have followed his example. Great archetypal stories like this tell us what to expect in the world, if we realize that the specific story points to patterns of grace always available, grace that has repeatedly been "made flesh" among us in lives as real as ours.

Adversity, as we have seen, can disrupt our personal stories and force us to revise them. The story of myself as Mrs. Draper's beloved Sunday school pupil was threatened by graduation into the intermediate department. Bob Clark's story of suburban family safety was run over and killed by a reckless driver. America's communal story of invulnerability to attack, safe behind two great oceans and its sense of special destiny, was punctured by the September 2001 attacks on New York and Washington. Martin's story of himself as a vigorous, healthy male was shattered by the onset of his disease.

Our task is then to "reframe" the difficult facts in a larger and more personal adequate story.[55] People do this with less distress when their overarching sacred story remains intact, providing themes and values to understand new experiences that, in turn, deepen understanding of the sacred story itself. There are hidden depths in these stories that only life-experience can reveal.

I could have claimed any one of a number of biblical adventure stories, said to myself, "God called Abraham to go to a new land," and moved into fourth-grade Sunday School, but I stuck with my old story of familiarity and missed that opportunity. Martin, before his death, knew he needed to piece together a larger story that could embrace both his suffering and the profound love he was feeling from family and friends. America still struggles in search of a larger framework to understand its harshly revealed place in the world.

Sometimes suffering shakes our belief in the sacred stories themselves, or at least our understanding of them. This whole book pivots on my discovery of the fresh meaning I found in the story of Jesus' suffering, meaning that helped me reframe my own approach to my difficulties. In order to see the Passion narrative as truly redemptive, I had to break free of the childhood interpretations I had absorbed and read the story afresh. One of the great sadnesses of the contemporary world is that of people rejecting the childhood version of their sacred Story without finding an adult perspective on their faith.

Throughout the ages, the story of Jesus' brave, compassionate, and redemptive mounting of the cross has had the power to speak in fresh ways, helping "reframe" the sufferings of millions in a redemptive context. I've seen it in many lives. In my parish ministry, we tried to give people such fresh perspectives through a contemporary Good Friday service each year for young people and their parents, using folk music and selections from *Godspell* and *Jesus Christ Superstar*. After one service, a mother came up to me with tears in her eyes. I knew that she was grieving about the difficulties her son was having in a life which was a far cry from the expected suburban story of success.

"I saw something so clearly this morning during that song about the Crucifixion," she said. "That man on the cross—that man is my son Neil. That's where he's at right now."

This great and true story had wrapped itself around her heart and changed her angle of vision about her son's life. And because she knew the end of the story, with its triumphantly empty tomb, she left crying not only tears of grief, but tears of hope as well.

To set your life in the context of Sacred Story, see Prayer Exercise 3 in the Appendix.

expecting God's help: from rescuer to resource

BATTLING RECURRENT CANCER CAN BE A daunting challenge to your story of self, world, and God. Facing an auditorium full of men and women battling recurrent cancer can also be daunting, especially if you're the one they're expecting to tell them how God can help them! They wouldn't be at this seminar if their fervent prayers for healing had resulted in a clean bill of health. Wariness is visible on many faces.

What am I to say to these people about God's presence and promises? How does this compassionate presence work "in all things for the good?" How can I fly under the radar of their wariness and invite a fresh openness to God?

I take a deep breath, utter an inward prayer, and hear myself say, "Some of us here may have been disappointed in our prayers because we expected God to rescue us from our difficulty. But God is not, primarily, in the rescue business. The biggest attitude shift you can make is from expecting God to be a *rescuer* to accepting God as a *resource*. God comes to us as available grace, 'grace to help in time of need,' as the New Testament book of Hebrews puts it."[56]

As I say it, the phrase "from rescuer to resource" sounds a bit flashy and pop for so serious a discussion. But it catches their attention. Some of the wary faces shift toward curiosity. The possibility of reframing their expectations about God is truly inviting to some of them.

As I continue speaking, I realize that the phrase really does capture the hard-earned lessons of my own ten-year wrestling match with the physical disease that caused my life-threatening depressions. (Dealing with this condition predated the emergence of the clear hum of emotional pain described in the Introduction.) Through this somewhat bitter struggle, I came to the realization that grace was truly available, always and everywhere, so long as I would accept, rather than demand the form in which that grace might appear. That acceptance, in turn, paved the way for the still later revelation, related in the Introduction to this book, that God could help me find a way out of the prison of emotional pain that lay buried underneath my periodic depressions.

facing the inevitable

While I would never deny that God can and does rescue people in some circumstances, there was no easy rescue from the suicidal depression that hit like a tidal wave in my thirtieth year. I had no idea that I suffered from a physical disease that translated itself into the periodic emotional tides that swept through me. Today my bipolar depression would be spotted right away, but thirty years ago that diagnosis wasn't widely used.

From my teens forward, I had learned how to survive the lows and ride the highs that rolled in periodically. After two or three months in the doldrums, feeling tired and sad and introverted, my mood would start to lighten, energy would take me out to other people, good humor would abound, and ideas would flow freely. This bright mood might last a few months or a year, but would always wane back into the gray twilight of sadness. In those darker days, prayer helped me through. Ignorant of the real causes, I figured the depression was some kind of character flaw or spiritual lack. Each time my abundant energy, creative ideas, and bold projects dissolved into sluggish disarray, I would examine my actions, look for the fatal flaw, repent of my lack of faith, and ask God to transform me into a person who wouldn't lose his nerve like this. Each time the depression passed, I was sure I had been rescued and that transformation was under way.

The much deeper depression of my thirtieth year was different. Suddenly, inexplicably, I didn't want to live any more. Vivid fantasies of ending my life in various ways occasionally gripped my consciousness. Did I really want to die? Why? The feelings didn't make any sense, and yet it was clear: I didn't want to go on. Nothing seemed to help. I couldn't concentrate enough to read or even watch TV. I was ashamed to be in groups because my mind was so sluggish I had difficulty responding in conversation. I was afraid to speak in public because I was sure everything I said was pure garbage—a severe disability for a preacher and teacher. My prayers fell with a thud into my own heart instead of connecting me with a sense of God. I really understood the plaintive voice of the Psalmist who laments that "darkness is my only companion."[57]

Not realizing that I was suffering from a biochemically induced disease, my therapist and I rummaged about in my psyche for the possible repressed anger he imagined caused my problems. At home, I searched frantically for divine deliverance: Maybe if I give up smoking, believe harder, deepen my prayer life . . . Psychologists call this the "bargaining" phase of dealing with a loss: If I do this or that, I can make it go away. If I'm just good enough, God will save me.

The short version of my bargaining phase is this: I prayed to Jesus to rescue me from the dark place, and no rescue came. In my most desperate moments, it seemed as if the Devil were laughing at the foolish credulity of my past faith. Slowly my faith dissolved into a confused fog. God was clearly not going to save me from facing this inevitability.

The psychotherapist and poet Gunilla Norris says that having to face one inevitability squarely is more fertile ground for spiritual growth than entertaining a thousand possibilities. Facing brute necessity unmasks all our childish fantasies and dashes our unrealistic expectations. We must deal with what is right there, blocking our path—the "boulder in the road," as she describes it.[58] In such a state, we may begin to accept the resources that are actually there rather than search vainly for the exit strategies we'd prefer.

Utterly defeated, I could only accept what was available: antidepressant drugs and a brief time of shelter from potential suicidal actions in the psychiatric ward of a nearby general hospital. Surrounded by people who were even more disturbed than I was, I realized that I must stand my ground rather than slide further into the pit of fear that threatened to swallow me up. Along with this realization came the stirrings of a small center of courage within me, like a muscle in the mind wanting to be exercised, inviting me to face my life a moment at a time, accepting what each moment brought. No one, not even God, could do this for me.

I had wanted God's rescue. Now I realized with some grimness, beggars can't be choosers. I needed to accept whatever goodness and grace, however small, might present itself in this bleak situation. My mind needed to feed on goodness rather than gnawing upon the dead and hollow sadness that filled me. The next day I began to take what came, step by step, looking for whatever goodness might be found: the smile of a nurse, dust motes dancing in the afternoon light, the visit of a friend.

In the twilight, as it were, one begins to see and be grateful for "small mercies." Without having the words for it, I had begun looking for resources rather than rescue. Though it didn't feel momentous at the time, this was the beginning of the courage to accept and deal with my condition. Courage, after all, isn't the absence of fear. Rather, it is the ability to act in spite of your fears, even if the only action possible is standing your ground, inhabiting the place and moment you are given, and accepting what is offered there.

Looking back on that time, I know that I was more richly supplied with resources than I realized at the time. Call it rescue if you must. It certainly didn't feel like that at the time. My therapist encouraged me to look on this as a "breakthrough rather than a breakdown." My mother- and father-in-law accepted their new son-in-law's distress with compassion and grace. My wife's love was brave and constant, and her dark humor occasionally jolted me into unexpected laughter. "What do you want out of life, anyway?" she asked one day. "What would it take to make you happy? You sometimes seem like a kid who thinks you can find it if you just climb the next mountain."

Out of my long years of idealistic piety I answered with St. Paul's ambitious line, "I want to grow up into 'the full stature of Christ.'"[59] Her eyes twinkled with a dark gleam, her mouth twisting wryly as she quipped back, "Couldn't you aim a little lower for starters?" After a startled moment, I began to laugh at the absurdity of confusing sainthood with ordinary happiness. I needed to begin where I was, rather than to expect the heights of spiritual perfection and emotional bliss.

Aiming "a bit lower" reinforced my decision to claim any available goodness: the freshness of a morning shower, the humor in a conversation with a fellow patient, the calmness that came from doing handicraft work, even the upbeat cheerfulness of the TV commercials I had always despised. The hopeful tag line on a popular sitcom's opening song, every week, promised me that "you're gonna make it after all." Small matters—the sorts of things I would have dismissed as insignificant or trivial a few months before. Then came the freedom of being released from the hospital, the feeling of wind and sunshine on my face, the returning sense of taste, the ability to appreciate a meal, my wife's encouraging touch, the ability to focus, read, and think, and the supportive presence of friends and family.

A few weeks after coming home, I had a momentary relapse. Though the antidepressants were taking hold, I still had bad days and better days. This day had been a bad one. Suicidal thoughts nibbled at the edge of my consciousness, and the black hole of despair threatened to open in the pit of my stomach. I fell "off the wagon," back into my inward pining for escape. Spiraling down into hopelessness, I threw myself face down on the bed and began weeping. This was a familiar, sinister path. I knew where it led, but I didn't seem able to stop. Suddenly, I had a sort of waking dream.

C. S. Lewis, whose no-nonsense approach to faith I had admired, was standing behind me puffing on a pipe. "Here, here, young man," he said, with compassion but great firmness. "This will never do. Buck up, buck up. Stop that right now. Go back down-stairs and play a game of cards with your wife!" This interrupted my hopelessness and offered me a choice. I tore myself away from the black hole within me, dried my tears, pasted a pallid smile on my face, went downstairs, and forced myself to play a game of cards with my wife. By the end of the game, I still felt miserable, but the black hole inside had closed. I had learned an important lesson: that muscle of courage inside could provide a balance to the uncontrollable sea tide of emotion.

There's a time and place for everything. Ordinarily, I would never simply say "buck up" to someone suffering clinical depression, which is quite different from "feeling low." That type of depression can't be cured by a shopping spree, a good movie, or a time of gratitude and praise. But at that moment, in that circum-stance, "buck up" was exactly what I needed to hear. I had lost touch with the muscle of courage without which we cannot face the situation we're in and find the resources in it, even if they are as meager as a game of pinochle. I now can see that God was fully present in that waking dream, tapping me on the shoulder as I cried, urging me, in Moses's words, to "choose life," not death.[60]

Once we have accepted that we must use all our powers to help ourselves, then we are in a position to use all the resources available to us, including divine assistance. This is one of the chief ways God works with us in any situation for the good. "God helps those who help themselves" is an American slogan, not a biblical verse. But the biblical idea is somewhat like it: God is able to help those who take what help comes their way and use it. Or as Paul puts it, "[W]ork out your own salvation with fear and trembling; for it is God who is at work in you."[61]

As I look back over the years, it is clear to me that a loving Divine Resource has led me into the wholeness I once thought impossible, first by giving me choices that led to a significant remission of the bipolar disorder, then to a long healing of the emotional pain hidden underneath it. The road to the Promised Land began, however, by learning how to survive in the desert.

discovering the divine resourcefulness

Of course, divine grace does appear to rescue us in some circumstances. I have heard direct testimony of deliverance from a wide variety of conditions. A man of my acquaintance was healed by prayer from macular degeneration of the retina, that slow-moving but ultimately devastating form of blindness. In my own ministry, I've known people whose cancer simply disappeared after healing prayer. I've read the mind-bending, fully documented before-and-after medical reports from the healing shrine at Lourdes. I've heard and read extraordinary tales of "angelic" rescue from disaster and danger.[62] There are plenty of people who say with King David that God "reached down from on high" and "delivered me from my strong enemy."[63] I know that grace can work in such amazing ways.

But I also know that these stories are extraordinary—quite precisely, extra-ordinary, not the ordinary way grace works. Though specific answers to prayer may sometimes come in startlingly precise ways, prayer is more about keeping open our connection with the Spirit's abundant goodness than it is about such results. I've ministered to more than one person who prayed fervently but was not healed of cancer. My northern New Jersey region is dotted with families whose loved ones were not angelically guided out of the collapsing World Trade Towers, however desperate their prayers may have been. The Christian healer who prayed for my friend with macular degeneration is himself permanently crippled and confined to a wheelchair.

Some people with enormous faith sicken and die. Those who demand a logically consistent overview of how grace works in every situation will be disappointed. Jesus was the agent for many miraculous answers to prayer and felt the guidance of the Spirit deep within. Yet the Gospels are not shy about reporting that Jesus himself came up against a seemingly solid stone wall in the most agonizing prayer of his life—"Father, let this cup pass from me."

At this pivotal moment, this prayer full of "loud cries and tears" did not receive the answer sought.

And yet the prayer does not fail, for prayer is about relationship more than results. The growing intimacy and trust of his relationship with God is revealed as he says, "Nevertheless, your desire, not mine be done."[64] As passionate as the specific desire may be, Jesus does not hold onto it covetously, but lets it go into the divine mercy, trusting that good will come, whatever happens on this dark twist of the road. His deepest desire is to be united with the flow of God's good work through the world, even if he does not understand at the moment.

As we walk the twists and turns of dealing with our difficulties, whatever they may be, grace appears as it appears. We should expect this. The Divine Mystery said to Moses, *ehyeh asher ehyeh,* which means not only "I am who I am" but "I will be who I will be," and even more radically "I will be where I will be. . . . I will be what I will be."[65] As Jesus puts it, the wind of the Spirit "blows where it chooses."[66]

What I've come to believe deeply is this: When I open a situation to be filled with the energy, light, and love of God, good comes. I can count on it. I just don't know beforehand exactly in what form that good will appear. Beggars can't be choosers. Jesus puts it a bit more gracefully, but just as starkly: "Blessed are the beggars."[67] Blessed are those willing to take whatever goodness they find and feed on it. Such willingness, he says, opens us to the "kingdom" or active rule of God, the moment-by-moment and day-by-day working of grace in our lives.

For Jesus, God is present with us, immediate and available. He sees God's goodness at work in natural processes, feeding the birds and clothing the fields with splendor. God's activity is subtle and silent, like yeast in rising dough. It sparks those "aha" realizations that come from the mysterious depths of the heart, like Peter's sudden realization that Jesus is Messiah. The Spirit's life-giving energy can bubble up through the inner core of our very own bodies. For him, nature and grace are not radically opposed, but are cooperating partners in mediating God's love.[68]

Such *ordinary* grace works *synergistically* with our own bodies, minds, and spirits, rather than crashing down from heaven like a thunderbolt. The Scriptures recognize this clearly. While some psalmists were rescued, others are *resourced* in the depths of their own being: "On the day I called, you answered me, you increased my strength of soul."[69] Like the Spirit brooding over the waters at the beginning of creation, God stirs up our powers from within.

the unexpected path of grace

The other thing I've come to believe is that, more often than not, God's grace guides and saves us *through* our difficulties, not *from* our difficulties. Most healings or resolutions of difficulty occur on levels where we didn't know we needed healing, and in ways we can't anticipate.

A young mother came to the holistic educational center I direct as she entered treatment for her third bout with breast cancer. A gregarious, fiery adventurer, Loris had decided to supplement her standard medical treatment with whatever alternative therapies might offer hope, and we offered mind-body meditation for wellness. Even though the odds were against her, she aimed at nothing less than complete remission for the sake of her husband and two young children. She was up for everything, anything that might help, and had already enlisted the aid of a prayer group at her Roman Catholic parish.

Not wishing to dent such enthusiasm, I nonetheless counseled her that neither an alternative nor a spiritual approach would guarantee a cure, but that good would surely come in some form. Still energetic in spite of her chemotherapy, Loris started taking yoga, using diet and supplements to compensate for the side effects of the medical treatment, spent time in meditative prayer, and joined a spiritual development group at our center.

In the end, the grace manifested in her journey came in forms that surprised us all. She didn't succeed in her original goal of "beating" the cancer, though she may well have prolonged her life by a year. But healing of other kinds abounded. "I don't know what else I'm getting out of this," Loris said a few months before her death, "but I now realize I'm on a soul-journey much more than a healing quest. I'm growing deeply in my relationship with God and other people, rather than just sinking deeper into my disease." And she wasn't the only one growing.

Loris's contagiously positive attitude and uncommon openness about her disease rallied people to her cause. People were free to relate to a real person in the presence of the disease, rather than being cowed into stunned silence or avoidance. Neighbors drove her to treatment and classes, rather than speaking to each other about her condition in the usual hushed tones of Northeastern suburban life. In the last few weeks, neighborhood children came and went in her home freely, stopping to say hello at her plant-surrounded bedside in the family room, and sharing in an ice cream party only days before her death. Her spiritual development class made a compact to join Loris in prayerful meditation at the same 10 PM time every night, wherever they were. Some of these meditators also helped her with periodic therapeutic touch, which eased her pain.

The transformation going on at the deepest levels of her self was palpable in the last days of her life. It was "as if layers were being stripped away so the essence shone through," according to her husband, Erik. As we prayed during my last pastoral visit to her, Loris's clear presence emerged, like a flower unfolding, in spite of the ravages of the disease and the influence of the heavy morphine. Suddenly this emaciated woman radiated beauty. As she looked slowly from person to person around her bed, the sense of intimate contact with her was powerful, and it seemed to me as if she were shining with a subtle, silver-gray light—or perhaps it was more than seeming. Her husband asked, later, if I had "seen that light around her." He had; and others had commented on the "powerful atmosphere." She died two days later during the regular 10 PM meditative prayer time, surrounded by family and cradled by the prayers of her friends.

Please don't think I'm romanticizing a grim death with talk about flowers, light, and beauty. Loris' body was destroyed by an aggressive and merciless disease, and she died in considerable discomfort, in spite of the palliative drugs. But the beauty we saw was real, too. We all witnessed that *simultaneous* presence of disease and abundant grace, ugliness and beauty, death and undying life which is part of life's mystery. Loris's journey taught me the meaning of what our forebears called a "good death." Her courageous choice to be open to the Spirit in her dying transformed her, the people around her, the way she walked her final days, and her last moments. Her tragic disease woven into a larger pattern of goodness, she was saved through her difficulties, not out of them.

Paradoxically, having settled for what seems like limited grace, one may come to realize that no limit can be set, in advance, on the unexpected richness of what may come, especially if one asks openly, in trust, for the Spirit to be our resource.

CHAPTER SIX

prayer in distress and disease

MY CHAPLAIN FRIEND KAY WAS STARTLED by the tangible sense of calm, clarity, and light in the room of the man dying of cancer. It was as if a radiance shimmered just out of visible sight. Discovering in the course of her visit that he was a monk who had practiced contemplative prayer regularly for decades, she commented on the atmosphere. "Well," he quipped wryly, "Contemplative prayer is all that keeps me going. Good thing I didn't wait for this thing to happen before I started practicing it."

Whatever "thing" we may face, prayer is meant to be our most immediate resource, because *prayer is our connection with the larger world of God's goodness that surrounds the narrow space of our difficulties.* The Spirit of life is directly linked to every soul on this planet, ready to help as allowed, but unwilling to violate our freedom and force grace on us.[70]

Prayer doesn't involve getting God to do something, but rather letting the Spirit flow freely through our lives. The divine generosity, which knows what we need before we ask, as Jesus tells us in the Sermon on the Mount,[71] doesn't need to be cajoled, bribed, or pleaded into responding. Whatever outer form our praying takes, it is always and everywhere a cooperation with the movement of God's Spirit already willing to help us, change us, and work through us. It is we who need to learn how to respond to the shimmering, sustaining, compassionate Presence which surrounds us always.

waking up out of habitual reactivity

I am repeatedly surprised at how far my ordinary consciousness seems to wander from this grace which is so very near. Tragically, our habitually defensive reactions to life's challenges create an alienated state of mind, and this only intensifies our sense of suffering. Late one gray, rainy winter afternoon I was returning home to New Jersey from a lecture in New York, annoyed and frustrated that subway delays had caused me to miss the hourly commuter train from Pennsylvania Station. Tired from overwork, the prospect of forty-five minutes "to kill" on such a dreary day was quite disgruntling. Muttering myself toward deeper misery, I turned into the Franciscan Church near Pennsylvania Station to calm myself. Twenty minutes of quiet did little to release the reactive tension my foolish overwork was breeding. Still annoyed at myself and at the world, I left the church and began to cross Seventh Avenue, the dark, wet asphalt of which seemed to echo and intensify my inner distress.

Silently and suddenly, in mid-stride, I was offered a choice—the choice of how to inhabit the moment. This was a reminder of what I had begun to learn so many years ago in the depths of my depression: I can resist or curse what is here, now, or respond with blessing. In fact, I am usually doing one or the other, consciously or unconsciously. The invitation was wordless, but clear: "Be here. Be open. *Let yourself be in God."*

So I did. On my next breath, I let go of the frustration and remembered the all-pervasive Presence. By an inner movement of the heart I began to allow the sights and sounds of the world to come in, rather than shutting them out in my agitation. My inner resistance broke. Astonishingly, between breaths the world changed all around me. I do not exaggerate. One moment I was encapsulated in my own colorless, dispirited reality; the next moment I found myself in God's own color-filled creation. The dreary gray light suddenly revealed itself as a silvery sheen. The wet asphalt glistened in the waning afternoon light, reflecting the colorful neon marquee of the train station. The many dozens of people nearby, whom I had scarcely noticed, loomed large in all their interesting variety, and I felt part of the tide of humanity moving through the streets. Once again, my life was "in God."

Prayer can help us remember, every time we forget, that God is the One in whom we "live and move and have our being," as the book of Acts tells us.[72] Our ordinary, preoccupied, reactive state of mind so often operates as if we were totally separate entities, surrounded by a capsule or border that separates us from the life around us. In that mid-stride moment I let the edge of my capsule become semi-permeable to the Spirit's life-connecting presence in and through all things. My cranky, self-imposed "suffering" disappeared like dew in sunlight, because it wasn't really suffering, just my own illusory sense of adversity. Even in cases of real adversity, the decision to open ourselves to the God-pervaded reality of the world rather than hunker down in our own separated space can make a decisive difference in how we experience the difficulty we're facing. Such willing surrender is the heart of prayer.

let suffering be in the presence of God

My colleague Jerry keeps slipping into the "half life," as he calls it, of chronic fatigue syndrome, a condition that continues to mystify both his doctors and the wellness therapists he's consulted. A man of vigorous intellect and spiritual curiosity, he's found that his ability to pursue the life of an active pastor has gradually diminished. He simply cannot muster the energy to carry the work load. "I have to guard my strength carefully," he says. "If I work too long, or push through the fatigue to do one more task, I pay for it with a more prolonged period of exhaustion and more physical pain than usual."

Over the past few years he's been drawn to what Christian tradition calls "centering prayer"—a simple, open, focused intention to be open to the divine presence.[73] Recently he's discovered that this contemplative prayer can be a gentle, effective way to bear with his periods of exhaustion. He didn't start at a contemplative level, however. He began by taking his pain to prayer.

"I've been trying to practice the pattern of the Psalms in my prayers," Jerry told me one day in a spiritual direction session.

"When I find myself getting cranky about the pain, I take my anger to prayer, and my complaints toward God. My problem is this: The Psalms begin with complaint and end with praise. How do you get to praise when you feel so lousy?"

After suggesting that praise might be too big a second step, I asked him if he ever "presented" his pain to God in contemplative prayer. I had been encouraging him for some time to offer to God whatever thought or feeling or sensation crossed his field of awareness during his silent prayer time. Now that I mentioned it, he did sometimes let his pain simply *be* in that openness to the Divine.

"What happens then?" I inquired. "Does it change how you're experiencing your discomfort?"

Yes, it did. "If I'm just focusing on my pain, it's the entire boundary of my experience. I'm inside of it. But when I turn to God, something bigger surrounds me. The discomfort somehow shrinks in size. The pain no longer bounds me because my sense of soul is bigger than it is. My fussing and anger dissipate, and I can rest in God. Somehow, this helps."

Without realizing it, Jerry had begun to practice one of the highest and simplest forms of prayer: the surrender of one's "bounded" self into the boundless reality of God. Such a "simple" act of prayer, however, isn't necessarily easy, because the human heart and mind know a thousand ways to distract themselves from the surrendered attentiveness.

How do we move from our ordinary habits of fussing resistance, anger, or downright cursing in the face of difficulty to such prayerful presence? Kay's monk knew the answer: practice—a practice that arises from the very ground of our difficulties and moves us gradually into a deepening sense of the Divine as "a very present help in trouble."[74]

Contemplative practice like this involves some or all of the following elements:

Recognize that the praying has begun already. Prayer, in the broadest sense, is always going on. We just don't call it that. From our earliest moments, something from deep down in our core wells up, wanting to reach out and *connect with something life-giving,* beginning with our first breath and our first sucking motion. When we find it, body and soul begin to purr. St. Augustine tells us he tasted God's goodness first at his mother's breast.[75] This natural, instinctual desire to reach out for nourishing goodness and rejoice in it is the root of prayer. We are intrinsically reciprocal, created to find and receive God's goodness, and give back gratitude. As we grow, the vocabulary of this natural, implicit prayer grows: Our gasps of delight and purrs of pleasure, our cries for help in distress, our outbursts of frustration, and the moans of our pain are, in this broadest and most natural sense, prayer, or at least the beginnings of it. In fact, our very groaning is part of the Spirit's work within us, stirring us to reach out for the divine goodness. As the medieval mystic Julian of Norwich hears God say, "I am the foundation of your beseeching."[76]

Of course, our natural instinct can lead us to less-than-profitable connections. We may reach out for soothing palliatives that offer no real life-power, drowning our discomforts in alcohol, smothering them with food, or distracting ourselves with amusements. Even in these diversions, our desire is to find something that seems good. The Spirit wants to help us find more satisfying and helpful forms of goodness, until we realize that God is the *summum bonum,* the supreme Good that includes all the goodness in creation.[77]

So, when faced with trouble, we can claim as prayer whatever pain, sorrow, outrage, discouragement, or desire we are already experiencing, presenting it to God. We can begin right where our difficulties discomfit us—with that fundamental desire to connect with life-giving energy in some form.

Connect consciously to the goodness of God. Even though this inborn prayer is a God-given ability, it grows through education and practice, like every other gift. Love, for example, arises spontaneously; but learning to love well is the work of a lifetime. This is why the disciples ask Jesus to "teach us to pray," even though they have been praying their whole lives.[78] I do not mean that God listens only to the highly skilled. Any genuine cry of the human heart surely resounds deeply in the heart of God. But learning how to overcome our habitual inattentiveness to the grace of God's surrounding goodness takes time and practice. Yet, as Julian of Norwich urges us, it is crucial that when we feel pain we should not obsess about it, but rather turn toward the "endless delight of God."[79]

Christian tradition, like Judaism, Buddhism, and every other spiritual pathway on the planet, has developed a wide range of spiritual exercises to open the heart to grace. In addition the more familiar forms of corporate worship, conversational prayer, and reading formal prayers from prayer books, there are methods that help shift our consciousness from their usual reactive, distracted state to a deeper connectedness with the Spirit's presence and power. The better part of wisdom is to practice a variety of the following prayer methods, and claim the ones that seem to help you best to connect with the Spirit's presence.

1. *Claim a sacred name or quality of God as a repeated "breath prayer."* This practice helps us savor deeply one particular aspect of the divine goodness at a time. Far from the "vain repetitions" Jesus warns about in the Sermon on the Mount,[80] this practice is designed to "anchor" the mind in awareness of God[81] by attentively repeating one of the thousand or more Names, adjectives, and phrases that reveal the many ways God works: *O Creator . . . Redeemer . . . Comforter . . . Christ . . . Spirit of life . . . love . . . peace . . . healing . . . courage.* The phrase can expand into a short prayer: *Spirit of life, enliven me.* Linking the phrase to the breath, or chanting it can help the mind focus more fully. The monks of the Eastern Church let this become a "prayer of the heart" by actively imagining the words coming from the "heart-space" in the core of the chest. Repeated choruses of praise or supplication can have the same effect as the use of the short prayer phrase.[82] This practice deepens the mind's ability to stay focused in the present moment without wandering, and can be good preparation for other forms of prayer.

2. *Use imagination rather than words.* Holding an image in the mind has great power to concentrate awareness. Imagination is as much a language of the soul as speaking. The well-known Ignatian Method of imagining oneself in a Gospel story is only one of many traditional imaginal prayer methods.[83] To immerse oneself in the radiant Light of God, or stand before Christ, can engage heart and mind deeply. The panoply of available images from Scripture and tradition is vast: We can invoke God as shepherd or king, father or mother. We can use natural images like mountain or rock, refreshing water, energizing wind, or radiant fire. We can imagine the "dazzling darkness" mystics say surrounds the splendor of God.[84] We can use these images as aids to savor the various qualities of the divine nature communicated by them, and let the sense of those qualities fill our awareness.

3. *Include the body in prayer.* The simple gesture of turning the palms upward in openness can invite an inner disposition to receptivity. We can bow in reverence, kneel in humility, or sit relaxed and attentive. Bodily movements both express and influence the heart. The body also has subtle, often undeveloped abilities to sense and respond to the energy of the Spirit at work in the life around us. As prayer deepens, one may become more sensitive to the quality of the life-energy or spirit-vitality in people, groups, places, and creation itself. We may feel the Spirit's healing and empowering flow quite distinctly. The body becomes a doorway to communion with the Spirit's reality manifest in all creation.

4. *Go beyond words and images into a wordless prayer.* Simple, full attentiveness to the God who is beyond all images is the main form of classical contemplative prayer. This practice was well-developed in the Judaism of Jesus' day and widespread in early Christian circles. The three other practices discussed so far train the mind to be present in the moment rather than carried away by distractions. Being here, now, simply open and receptive, becomes possible. After using a word, image, or gesture to point the mind toward God, one lets it go and remains still with only a

bare intention toward God. This wordless "centering" prayer is what Jerry was practicing, being present to God, pain and all. This bare intention toward God, long practiced, is what opened the depths of the suffering monk to the shimmering light that sustained him. The intention to connect with God is the very heart of any spiritual practice. The goal is not the production of a specific state of feeling, much less a mystical rapture, but openness to the divine reality that surrounds, pervades, and sustains us.

present yourself and all that is in you.

"Here am I" is one of the most basic prayers of the Bible.[85] In his acute fatigue, all Jerry can do is let his pain "be" in the Presence. God, of course, does not need to be informed about our pain. But we need to "present yourselves to God," as St. Paul urges the Roman Christians.[86] Like opening a wound to the cleansing power of air and light, or crying on the shoulder of a friend, we let our inner reality be exposed to God's love.

This means everything—aches, pains, gripes, urges, and desires—not just our loftiest aspirations. All the background muttering needs to be brought into the light: *"Oh, this hurts. . . . I wish it would stop. . . . That my sister-in-law would shut up . . . That the surgery will be successful."* Joys as well as needs can be turned to conscious prayer: *"What a glorious day! . . . Umm, wonderful strawberries . . . I'm so grateful for this friendship."*

As we have already noted, our moans and groans, even our most unworthy desires, are already prayers of a raw, primitive sort. All these, as well as our desires and delights, need to be given breathing room in light of God's love so they can be cleansed, clarified, and "uncramped." Our mind tends to tense around a need or desire, cramping it with the intensity of a small child wanting exactly what it wants when it wants it. Our raw desires easily turn into painful cravings, intensifying our misery if we don't get what we want—now![87]

Desire is meant to mature into a motivating force propelling us toward all the good that God offers us. We are invited to risk releasing our desires into the merciful and compassionate keeping of a God who is seeking to do "more than all we can ask or imagine," as the writer of Ephesians assures us,[88] but in ways that may not fulfill our initial expectations. By presenting our desires to God, we can let them become *open-ended desire*—desire without the demand for immediate fulfillment. We may discover that some desires are changed into a yearning for something more basic and real than we thought we wanted at first. As we present the energy of our desires, God can work with them like a potter with clay, crafting and shaping them. We may want to be released from the dispute we're having with fellow-workers, for example, whereas Divine Wisdom sees in this dispute the opportunity for us to learn how to handle conflict more effectively.

Likewise, we tend to hold onto our delights for dear life, wanting them to last, determined to repeat the experience. Held so tightly, delight becomes the prelude to loss. By presenting our delights to God as gratitude and praise, we can enjoy and then let go, leaving ourselves ready for the next grace that will cross our path.

receive available grace

"Open-ended" desire can help us be ready for the grace that actually comes to meet us in this circumstance, at this stage of our journey, rather than pining for what we do not have.

In the depths of my suicidal depression I pined for release, but found, instead, unanticipated gifts—many of them not appreciated at the time. The first grace I received, as I look back on it, was the clear moment of sanity when I realized I had to enter the hospital and acknowledge I could not deal with the depression without medication. Only then could the long, circuitous course of soul-mending begin that would lead to healing.

As I mended, I discovered that while prayer might not cure all ills, praying through the recurring emotional storms made me aware of something deeper in me than emotion, deeper even than "personality"—a reality of the deep self that is a steadying power through upheavals, and the place from which we can open ourselves to God most profoundly.

One doesn't have to have a major crisis to encounter in prayer such unexpected, but freely available grace in prayer. My friend Mark was very devoted to leading services with a hearty enthusiasm. "After all," he says, "the Eucharist is the 'Great' Thanksgiving of the Church, and I felt it was my responsibility to help inspire enthusiasm in the congregation." One Sunday, he just couldn't muster the energy. Recent events had left him quite discouraged. At the altar, he simply offered himself to God and said the prayers as written in his church's liturgy. "I said those prayers from my hurt, apathy, and hopelessness because I really couldn't do anything else." Much to his astonishment, the people were deeply affected, some moved to tears by the beauty of the service. Instead of being a cheerleader, Mark had actually presented himself to God, and thus opened himself to become the channel of that good Spirit who can do surprising things with whatever is offered. Mark's experience left him more able to trust the grace of God to lead worship through him, rather than relying simply on his own energy and enthusiasm.

Experiences like these are part of the soul's *askesis,* or training. God is in the business of soul-making, and is able to use every difficulty, disease, and adversity as part of the process of growing us into real partnership with God, and cooperation with the streams of grace moving through the world. This does not mean that adversity is necessarily arranged by God, who does not "willingly afflict or grieve anyone," as the writer of Lamentations affirms.[89] On the contrary, whatever happens, no matter what the cause, can become grist for the mill of our growth, most powerfully when it is "presented"—accepted, offered, and worked with.

cultivate appreciation, thanksgiving, and blessing

God does not send adversity so we can appreciate life more by contrast, but adversity does often intensify a sense of what is precious in life. During the terrible siege of Sarajevo, when snipers made venturing outdoors in daylight perilous, the nights were filled with throbbing music as people gathered in basement discos and cafes to drink, dance, laugh, and, most of all, spend time in each other's company. While there was surely some desperation behind the gaiety, they were claiming whatever "bread in the wilderness" they could find. As countless people living with life-threatening disease testify, the threat of death can heighten appreciation of the simple things in life and open our eyes to the surprises of grace.

Any desert is alive with life for those who have the eyes to see it. The children of Israel, blinded by their constant complaining about the trials of their wilderness journey, were surrounded by unexpected and unappreciated grace: water from a rock, a great feast from the unexpected visitation of a flock of quail, and the discovery that a desert plant secreted by night a gooey juice that dried in the morning sun to a white, flaky "bread" that proved both sweet and nourishing.[90]

One of the most contented people I've ever met is a woman whose husband died suddenly, leaving her and three small children virtually destitute. Alone, without anyone to turn to, the person I'll call Maria decided to "abandon" herself in trust to the providence of God and accept what came with gratitude. Of course she did her part, looking for work, getting job training, and caring for her kids; but times were very tough. Yet she arose each day choosing to look for the blessings in it. Lacking money for Christmas presents, she made a game out of leading her children in creating colored-paper gifts for each other and inventing games to make the holiday festive. Shopping at second hand shops for clothing, Maria involved the kids in "searching for the finest available" not only for themselves, but for each other. In time she found ever-better jobs, and today enjoys sufficient financial resources for her family, but her experience taught her not only gratitude for every gift and grace, but trained her to see the possibilities rather than the limitations in any situation. The fruit of this was a grateful heart.

Sometimes these possibilities present themselves, unbidden, as sheer grace. One of my deepest and most lasting experiences of God happened during one of my depressions. I was not so much in despair as in a kind of quiet emptiness. Slowly, I came to realize that I could use this unfamiliar inner stillness to be present and receptive to any situation without the distracting mental clutter of my elated periods. As I walked one day into our dining room, a shaft of bright August light ricocheted off a leaf of the mock orange bush just outside the window and splashed into my left eye. The blast of light evoked something deep within me, and for one utterly endless moment I knew with every cell of my being that my life, and all our lives, were rooted in the eternal light and life of God which I now glimpsed inwardly.[91] Even as the moment passed and I was delivered back into the subdued emptiness of my current condition, my heart hummed with thanksgiving for this assurance. Sharing this experience with a friend who was "raw and bleeding" from divorce helped him realize that he too, while not subject to such mystical moments, was "more porous" in his grief to the smell of the summer earth and the comforting sound of the cicadas in the night.

What we call praise arises out of appreciation of such experiences, from the delight we learn to take in creation, and the gratitude we feel in response to events that give form to God's goodness. This recurrent delight is so strong that, for most people, few adversities have the power to take it away permanently, and our hearts rise to gratitude and praise of their own bidding, sometimes to the mystification of our minds.

we are never without resources

In prayer we can rediscover, again and again, that we are never alone, never disconnected, never without resources. Reciprocity is at the heart of every breath, every bite of food. We cannot fall out of God, in whom we live, and move, and have our being. Some measure of God's goodness is available to us, even in the deepest pit of the darkest hell. Indeed, Christ, who "descended into hell," as the Apostles' Creed says, is the sign and seal of a wise compassion that has experienced such hells itself, and has walked the pathway through them unconquered to that larger life that surrounds us and will hold us in its power forever.

To "present yourself" and others to God, and to invest in the "treasury of the heart," see Exercises 4 and 5 in the Appendix.

CHAPTER SEVEN
finding joy whatever happens

PARADOXICALLY, LEARNING *HOW* TO
suffer is the secret of finding joy in the midst of suffering. One of
life's strangest discoveries is joy's ability to coexist with emotions that
seem to contradict it. I've listened to people deep in grief speak of
loved ones who have died and heard the joy of their love humming
beneath the sobs. I've faced challenges that laced my heart with
fear, yet sensed a fierce joy for life itself underneath my fear.

This is because joy, properly speaking, is not so much an emotion
as it is a way the heart is disposed toward life itself. In fact the
word "joy" itself can fill us with exaggerated expectations of bliss.
Perhaps "a sense of connection with goodness" would be better. "I
would have lost heart," sings the psalmist, "unless I had believed
that I would see the goodness of the LORD in the land of the
living."[92] People are often surprised to discover such a connection
in odd and unhappy circumstances.

One of the moments of surprising joy in my young adult life
came in the midst of terrible rage at a good friend who had
betrayed an important confidence. This rage, simmering out of
conscious sight, started coming out one evening as we jokingly
spoofed some characters we had just seen on the satirical TV comedy
"Batman." Taking the part of the villain, I playfully started to
chase my friend down the campus through the deepening twilight,
shouting, "I'll make you pay, Batman." Soon the friend I'll call Chad
found himself cornered on a ledge overlooking a deep, rock-filled
moat. He saw in my eyes something that wished him harm. "My
God," he said, "you look like you could kill."

As he spoke the words, I knew they were true. We were alone. I could do him real harm—and something in me really wanted to. But in that same moment, I also knew that I wouldn't. Not only had "Thou shalt do no murder" written itself into my heart, but I knew that my rage was injured friendship, a bond deeper than wrath. A complex swirl of joy washed over me: joy over both my ferocious passion and the protective commandment that held it firm in its God-given grip; joy in the feeling of physical ability to harm, but also to defend and protect; and joy at feeling, quite simply, part of the human race, blessed and burdened with the same passions as everyone else, however dark and dangerous some of them might be. Sheer goodness, all of it. The rage dissolved in this flood of joy. Apologies were offered, and our friendship was wrapped in an even deeper bond.

Such joy is very different from happiness, even though the dictionary links them closely. Happiness depends, as the derivation of the word implies, on happenstance, on what's happening, over which we usually have little control. We can sometimes make ourselves happy just by arranging circumstances that stimulate good feelings.

Joy, on the other hand, cannot be manufactured, and does not necessarily depend on circumstance. Joy can arise anytime, anywhere, if the heart is disposed toward goodness. And since God dwells in everything that is good and true, joy is one of the surest signs of God's presence within us, as St. Teresa of Avila knew.[93] That connection can help sustain us through anything.

How can we train the heart to connect with that joy, whatever the circumstances? We can do so only if we forswear happiness as our goal, let go of our resistance to circumstances, invest in the "treasury of the heart," and remember that our lives are always lived within the spaciousness of God's own life.

do not make happiness the goal

Try as hard as we might to achieve "life, liberty, and the pursuit of happiness," most lives are filled with a number of unhappy circumstances, small or great. Cars get stuck in traffic jams, spouses get up on the wrong side of the bed in the morning, children misbehave, the boss is cranky or unfair, cherished friends move away, youthful dreams are sometimes never realized, and physical ailments creep into most lives, sooner or later. Expecting happiness to be a God-given right is a setup for disappointment.

"Whoever told us we're supposed to be happy all the time?" said my colleague Geoffrey, a member of a support group of young clergy just setting out in ministry many years ago. He'd suffered a professional disappointment, and was the new father of an infant keeping him awake too many nights. "We've been sold a bill of goods!" he thundered, inveighing against the onslaught of television commercials and slick magazine ads promising a paradise of happiness through career and consumerism. While a bit overwrought, he was right. Modern citizens of economically advantaged countries have been filled with expectations most human beings through the centuries would find astonishingly unrealistic.

The ancients, biblical folk included, expected the happiness of life to be laced with adversity and sorrow as a matter of course. The biblical sage we call "the Teacher" tells how he sought happiness in every possible way: through wealth, sensuality, and knowledge. The harder he tried, the more he discovered the impermanence of pleasures, which rise and fall with circumstance. As he writes in *Ecclesiastes,* he came to accept that "for everything," both pleasant and unpleasant, life-giving and death-dealing, "there is a season."[94] Rather than strive for happiness, he counsels, accept what comes and cherish the good things: "Light is sweet, and it is pleasant for the eyes to see the sun. Even those who live many years should rejoice in them all." Yet, he counsels, "[R]emember that the days of darkness will be many."[95] Such expectations are similar to the ancient Greek sense of "moderation in all things" and Eastern teachings about the impermanence of life current in the Teacher's day, but their sober balance feels starkly gloomy to many readers today.

Modern people are not supposed to be unhappy. The modern worldview is a strong reaction to ancient soberness and a studied rejection of medieval pessimism. Medieval life had its triumphs and joys, of course, but a sense of life more tragic than the ancient classical and biblical one prevailed, expressed in gloomy hymns like Bernard of Morlaix's "Brief life is here our portion."[96] The modern determination to pursue earthly happiness arose after a long period of troubles, including the fall of the Roman Empire, the barbarian invasions, the Black Death and the Reformation's wars of religion. Through science and technology, education and industrial progress, democracy, and the kinder, gentler style of civil behavior we call "humaneness," modern people have sought to create a happier world. To some extent we have succeeded: Economic development, medical progress, and increased personal freedom to pursue their dreams do give people the power to create better circumstances. This inventive, "get up and go" society has created enormous earthly good in the world for millions of people. Even the sober, old biblical Teacher seems to support this aspect of the modern mood when he says, "Whatever your hand finds to do, do with your might."[97]

Yet I'm sure the Teacher would be the first to point out that all this "progress" has a dark side, creating new opportunities for unhappiness. Lower infant mortality rates lead to population growth, which leads to environmental degradation and more people to face starvation when famine comes. Better health leads to longer lives, and this leads to more sufferers from senile dementia and Alzheimer's disease. Having too many choices, even of good things, seems to breed more dissatisfaction as people wonder if they've chosen the best product or career. Unhappiness is an inevitable part of earthly life, and the modern dream of creating a trouble-free earthly paradise is an illusion.

Please don't think I'm against happiness. I've known a good measure of it in my own life, and wish happy circumstances for as many people as possible. But to make it one's primary goal, as my colleague Geoffrey saw so clearly in his early thirties, is a setup for disappointment, even if you succeed. As one highly successful businessman said to me, "Now that I've brought home not only the bacon, but the whole pig, I should be happier. Where can I find something that will give me joy?"

Even making joy the goal is ill-advised, for joy cannot be manufactured. We are called, rather, to make connection with goodness our aim, and aligning our lives with God's purposes our goal, no matter what happens. From this perspective, there are constructive uses even for unhappiness. As an urban minister, Geoffrey has found much to be unhappy about: low-income workers forced out of gentrifying neighborhoods; workfare mothers whose minimum wage jobs will never pay as much as welfare did, whose children now have no medical coverage; ordinary citizens up against a city hall deaf to their complaints about neighborhood problems. His unhappiness has organized effective campaigns to meet these needs. His joy, when it comes, is a by-product of determined anger at injustice, driving zeal for reform, and unsentimental concern for human well-being. He still fumes over a cultural cult of happiness that turns people's eyes away from the needs of the poor and disadvantaged, as well as the shadow side of our own lives. Because he accepts that some things are really as bad as they seem, he is able to respond in ways that make a difference in the world.

let go of resistance

Though acceptance of the way things are is key, it is easier talked about than done. As we face some threat, however small, we may well go through resistance, denial, anger, catastrophizing, and hunkering down before the letting-go of real acceptance sets in. There is no adversity human beings face that can't be made worse with a little effort, and resistance is the first step.

We can start by avoiding the problem as long as possible, for example. We may feel afraid and helpless, so we avert our gaze. A woman discovers a lump in her breast but doesn't call the doctor. "What if it's cancer?" she thinks, her mind turning quickly away. A man suffers recurrent chest pains. "If this is my heart, I could die," he fears, and turns on the TV to find something pleasant to think about. Parents suspect their kid is taking drugs, but minimize what they are seeing. "Was he stoned, or is it just our imagination?" they ponder, deciding that he is, after all, a good kid and they can trust him. Avoidance, if practiced, quickly becomes outright denial. Denial is a major human enterprise, often putting off the reckoning until the situation is much worse.

When the doctor told me I had high blood pressure my response was anger at him and scorn for his suggested medication. The insane strategy of my denial was mind-boggling. How could I have high blood pressure, with all my deep meditation? How dare he suggest medication when there was surely some natural, holistic fix? Just who did he think he was dealing with? It took some time and an alarming echocardiogram for this delusional bubble to burst. In spite of weight loss, exercise, acupuncture, deep massage, relaxing meditation—and even prayer—my high blood pressure didn't yield. Fortunately, the dreaded medication seems to work just fine, without any significant side effects.

Why was I so angry? What possessed me to prove the doctor wrong? Resistance is, sadly, one of the forms of ordinary madness we human beings use to block out what we don't want to see.

When we finally acknowledge the facts, we may still see them with judgmental, defensive eyes, giving the most negative spin to any situation. Negative spin can subtly enter into how we see life every day. "What terrible weather! Isn't it awful?" Dottie exclaims as she bustles into my regular Wednesday seminar. She doesn't mean she's been chased by a tornado or drenched by a typhoon, just that it's raining. Such inaccurate, negatively spun speech may seem a small matter; but maybe the reason Jesus calls us to be aware of "every idle word"[98] is that our words quietly and inexorably shape how we see the world. Psychologists call Dottie's rather common way of reacting "catastrophizing." Jargon though the word may be, it's an apt description of how the hyped-up language of news broadcasts seeps into our daily speech patterns, inviting us to see life as a nightmare.

Jesus faced difficult situations with clear eyes, compassionate eyes that accept what's there and search for what's needed. "See clearly what is before you," says Jesus in an early Christian version of his sayings.[99] If you're setting out for a battle, he teaches in Luke, you'd better assess what you're up against and see what resources you need to meet it.[100]

As we turn to face any problem, however, one final hurdle to potential joy remains: our understandable tendency to hunker down and focus exclusively on the problem. We may be lost in a swirl of obsession and worry, fall into despondency, or simply feel unable to see beyond the confines of our difficulty. Life sometimes simply swamps us. The compassionate love of God knows "how we were made" according to Psalm 103,[101] and even "falls with us" into our wretchedness, in order to help us find our way through and out, according to the medieval visionary Julian of Norwich.[102]

invest in the treasury of the heart

That larger world of grace sometimes surprises us out of our misery by its grace. A parishioner woke early one morning lost in stewing about some minor difficulties with his wife, and took the dog for a walk rather than sit and sulk. The dark, cloudy morning, still wet from late night rains, matched his dour mood perfectly. Just as he was beginning to fret even more because of this unhappy match of inner and outer weather, his path through the woods took a turn into the sunlight breaking through the clouds, creating a perfect rainbow. Bedazzled into joy by the rainbow, he was invited inwardly to let go of the fussing. One long slow breath of release later, "things were back in perspective." The unhappiness did not disappear, but was displaced from the center to the sidelines of his attention, and he began to see his situation from a new perspective. He was restored to a saner place in God's world.

What surprises us by grace needs to be claimed in faith and practiced. My friend Ellen, who was saved from despair by the grace of sunlight shining through a droplet of water, taught me how to invest in what Jesus calls "the good treasure of the heart," from which such memories of good can be brought when needed.[103] "Make a storehouse of memories," she says, "and bring them out to savor in difficult moments." Remembered grace can help keep us from getting stuck in reactivity, bring us back into the larger world, and create enough perspective to see the actual goodness in a situation.

My struggle with depression drew me often to the ocean for comfort. I loved to sit and watch the sunrise turn the Atlantic Ocean into a blaze of rippling light. I ate the light; I drank it; I soaked it up like a sponge. And I set the narrow darkness of my depression into the open greatness of that sparkling sea. The images became a part of a treasury of my heart, ready to bring out in moments of need, a symbol of the divine light that St. John says the darkness cannot overcome.[104] To this day, it is the central symbol of God for me, invoked to surround me in any difficulty.

remember the spaciousness

God's love is the vast spaciousness that surpasses and surrounds all the narrow places of our lives. No matter how small our confines may be, we can always remember and breathe from this vastness. A woman who suffers from claustrophobia does exactly this when the walls are closing in around her. Samantha slows her breathing, closes her eyes, and imagines a far horizon under a vast sky. With each breath, she imagines inhaling God's clean, fresh air all the way from that far horizon. By so doing, she invites her feeling of illusory confinement to let go into the real dimensions of the space she's inhabiting.

The space we are always inhabiting is the "midnight sky" I saw in Jesus' heart on Palm Sunday so many years ago. It has the power to deliver us, like him, from the fear that can hinder consciousness of our connection with God. The psalmist exclaims, "When I am afraid, I put my trust in you."[105] "The real gift, " said a friend I'll call Art, "is the dispelling of fear, not suffering." A heart ruled by fear cannot easily receive the gift of joy.

I needed to remember this spaciousness on one of my last trips to visit my dying father. My dad's explosive temper and wounding sarcasm remained a challenge, in spite of some measure of compassion that I had for the inner unhappiness in him that fueled these outbursts, I was nonetheless justifiably on guard, and armed myself all the way on the plane with a breath prayer: "May my heart be filled with your loving-kindness, may I be easy and at peace, may I know your goodness." The prayer continued as I joined my father and a cousin who had come to relive memories of their childhood on the farm in Kentucky. All through the weekend, the prayer returned to root me in memories of God's loving-kindness, allowing me to deal with my father compassionately.

Just as things were going swimmingly, my father, buoyed up by kind attention and an old-fashioned country meal, loosed a characteristic barbed arrow aimed at spoiling the moment. My old reaction of feeling closed in by this oppression stirred. I made an excuse to step outside for a moment, breathed deeply, and remembered the surrounding love of God. This brought the prayer for compassion up again out of the treasury. As I returned to the room, my glance fell on the redness of the strawberries in the bowl my cousin had just set on the table. Reaching out, I picked one, took a bite, and savored the sweetness filling my mouth. The cross-section of the half-eaten strawberry, with its starburst pattern in white, rose, and red, suddenly seemed one of the most beautiful things I had ever seen in my life. Joy arose spontaneously. As my father's patter continued, zigzagging from ordinary chatter to zings of grumbling, I was filled with a sense of the goodness at the center of life. For the rest of the weekend, this joy was the bass note under all discordant notes.

When we refuse to pin all our hopes on happiness, learn how to let things be instead of resisting what happens, we can inhabit the only space where joy is possible: here and now. Cultivating a rich treasury of good memories helps us, in this moment, to remember and realize that God is as constantly present as the groundwater, as available as the air, as dependable as the sunlight, ready to well up into our hearts at the slightest touch of goodness. Learning how to be present and available to that goodness is the habit that opens us to a treasure Jesus himself knew how to find and share: joy that no circumstance has the power to take away.[106]

blessed be the goodness

Blessed are you, compassionate Source
of our living and our dying,
the Wellspring of our days,
in whose shelter the sinews of our bodies
and the shape of our souls come to be;
in the boundary of whose love
we learn to dream, and know, and love
what is good, and seek it,
and in the limits set for us,
small and great, both easy and harsh,
are invited to choose life, and love it.

Blessed be the goodness we find,
and the difficulties that grow us.
Blessed be the length of our days,
and the shortness of them,
calling us to cherish each hour,
and create each day
with deeds of loving-kindness.

Blessed be the Greater Life
of which we are a part,
the surging tides of air and water
that fuel this green planet's life;
the sweep of humankind through the ages,
upon whose shoulders we stand,
the power of those who have
waded through the vale of tears
and found it full of living water.

Blessed be the mystery of Eternity
in which our little lives are remembered
and held deep in your loving Heart.

PART THREE

fellowship in suffering

compassionate presence:
how to be better than Job's friends

WHEN HER NEPHEW'S LIFE WAS CUT
SHORT in his mid-twenties by a plane crash, Sister Madonna felt
entirely unprepared to help her family deal with the loss. Flying
from New York to West Virginia, the Franciscan nun fretted about
what she could say to her sister. Surely a professionally trained,
officially "religious" person should know just the right words to
bring comfort, encouragement, and faith.

"Any possibility of words evaporated the moment I stepped into
the funeral home," she told the congregation at a parish mission I
attended. "My sister stood by her smart, promising son's casket."
Helplessly, her own tears starting, Sister Madonna strode across
the room and embraced her sister. They held each other wordlessly,
weeping together. Her sister later thanked her for those endless,
tear-filled, wordless minutes. "I couldn't have borne any words of
comfort from you," she told Madonna, "especially anything about
God. I just wasn't ready."

Such silent compassion arises naturally when hearts and lives are
truly linked, as were those of the Franciscan sister and her family.
In such moments we don't need advice or philosophy, but someone
to hold us, quietly and tenderly.

The word compassion means, literally, "enduring-with, feeling-
with, undergoing together." We are not made to be alone in suffering.
"Jesus wept" with Mary and Martha when their brother died.[107]
How others are present, or not present, to us can actually influence
our future well-being. People who have good social support when

difficulty strikes are likely to adjust more easily and recover more quickly than people who are isolated.[108] Other people can help us move through our fear, anger, or grief—all innate responses of body and soul to adversity—in ways that help heal the wounds.

I first experienced the power of the "good grief" that Sister Madonna helped flow when I attended my grandmother's country wake. Old customs were still alive in rural Tennessee in the early 1980s. Near my grandmother's open coffin women stood sobbing while men's eyes teared up in their stoic farmers' faces. Only a few feet away old friends cracked jokes or jawed about cotton prices while relatives greeted one another warmly. These Scots-Irish folk still knew how to have an old-fashioned wake: The circle of grief and death was surrounded by a bigger circle of warmth and life. Hearts softened and opened by grief, people drew together to feel each other's aliveness in the face of death.

I had the most vivid image as I stood there: Grandmother's death was a wound in all of us; this gathering was the bloodstream of life itself, bathing that wound with love. My grief could flow freely in this larger, healing flow. We grieved, sustained by a barely noticed joy underneath it all, and celebrated the cycle of living and dying.

Compassion may rise naturally in such circumstances, but there is always a choice involved. I've been to "viewings" that were just that: People were onlookers, tightly guarding their feelings, rather than fellow-sufferers. Even going to a wake requires us to transcend our own fears. We can say "yes" to sharing-in-suffering, or defend ourselves from the discomfort of "undergoing together."

being present —and the instinct to avoid it

The friends of Job—the Bible's archetypal figure of suffering humanity—are themselves typical of the human instinct to protect ourselves against the nearness of suffering. They hide from the impact of Job's suffering on themselves by a variety of subterfuges— avoiding emotional presence, dispensing platitudinous advice, and running at the mouth rather than listening with the heart. The suffering of the world needs better companioning than these friends offered Job. How can we be more compassionate than Job's friends?

Most importantly, we can offer our presence, and not fall into avoidance. Compassion like Sister Madonna's requires being truly present to the sufferer. Sister Madonna could have tried harder to stay "in control" for the sake of being "helpful." She could have stayed safe behind her professional image, pretending to be serene and calm in the midst of raw emotion. Had there been some unhealed wound in the relationship with her sister, she might have even withheld her love, refusing to bypass her own wound to tend to the pain of others. The strategies human beings find to protect themselves against being present to, much less sharing in the pain and sorrow suffering brings, are many and varied.

Sue, one my fellow participants in a spiritual companionship group, felt "betrayed, shamed, and abandoned" when she was abruptly terminated from her position, apparently for political reasons. "My isolation and shame were made worse by the fact that people I had worked closely with ignored me. They acted as if I had a disease they might catch." The plunge from feeling confident and productive at the peak of her career to feeling "nailed" was devastating.

The abandonment Sue experienced is all too commonplace. Many of us flee not just death, disaster, or disadvantage, but the slightest hint of them. Flocks of geese will ostracize a sick goose. Bands of chimpanzees will shun a chimp who is emotionally disturbed. Some human beings abandon even loved ones in the face of serious or prolonged illness. The raw instinct to survive can develop into refined strategies for self-protection and avoidance, protecting us from the pain of the situation.

Psalm 69 speaks poignantly about the effect of such avoidance, in words made familiar by Handel's *Messiah:* The sufferer "looked for some to have pity on him, but there was no man, neither found he any to comfort him."[109] Christ knew this suffering as his followers abandoned him to trial and crucifixion, fearing for their own lives. Remarkably, as Sue moved through her hurt to reflection, she "remembered the times I myself had felt helpless in the face of another's suffering. I guess they just didn't know what to say or do." Still, all she needed was someone to hear her story, "just hear it without judgment. That would have made a big difference. Even a simple 'I'm so sorry' would have gone a long way."

We need to become more aware of our own fears if we wish to behave compassionately. I realized, as a young pastor making hospital calls, that I could always find a dozen other things to do, delaying hour after hour my hospital visitations. Realizing this was the pattern, I began exploring the shape of my inner reluctance, even as I forced myself through the hospital door. The feelings were not very far from the surface: I was threatened by sickness. As I walked down the corridors the telltale odor of sick bodies seeped through the hospital's antiseptic smell. This reminder, in flesh so near to my own, of my own potential helplessness in the face of disease and death, made me profoundly uneasy. Once aware of this, I could face it more courageously, present my fear to God, call on the Spirit's support, and let myself be more present to the patient.

the power of simple presence

Sometimes, simply being present is all that is needed, as Sister Madonna knew instinctively. In our initial reaction to adversity, the last thing most of us need is somebody spouting pious platitudes about the reasons we may be suffering, offering bracing advice, or telling us it's not as bad as we think. I've known people who tell someone with suicidal feelings that they "don't really mean it," others who try to dissuade a drinking buddy from admitting his alcoholism, and still others who freely offer the pious old bromide that "it's God's will."

Job's friends are the Bible's chief examples of the impulse to control our fears by imposing meaning hastily. Job has been their ideal of the righteous man. If such a noble person has lost everything—property, wealth, family—it could happen to anyone. They are afraid to empathize with his suffering, because if they do they will have to admit that what befell Job could also happen to them.

To give them credit, they join him in the silence of his mourning for many days. But the first time the anguished man breaks the silence with a cry of utter despair—"Why did I not die at birth?"—the friends cannot wait to correct him. What has happened to him shakes their view of reality, which must now be defended at any cost. Their cascade of "little reasons" for suffering lasts for many chapters. Job must have sinned. He's arrogant and proud. His sin is proved by his resistance to their theology. But it is they who are resisting the simple reality of Job's pain. Real compassion takes courage, the courage to face things as they are without trying to put a self-defensive spin on it.

Such unsolicited help is seldom helpful, even when correct. Sue wanted simple inquiries about her well-being rather than unsolicited advice when she lost her job; at most "some help in thinking things through, if I'd asked." The compassionate friend stands ready to respond to the sufferer's expressed needs.

A woman I'll call Janet was blessed to find just such a friend when she realized her alcohol problem. "I was literally setting out the glasses for a cocktail party when it dawned on me," Janet told our sharing group. "I saw myself, in my mind's eye, having too much to drink yet once again, and I realized this was out of control." Providentially, Janet's neighbor, a drug and alcohol counselor, had already demonstrated a sympathetic ear. In that graced moment, Janet picked up the phone, called the neighbor, and blurted out her realization. The woman made a simple suggestion: "Let's go to an AA meeting." "Now? With this party about to begin?" "They'll have a fine time with your husband," was the response. "There's a meeting in half an hour I'd be happy to attend with you."

Janet is grateful for her neighbor's willingness to hear the real plea behind her overt words. She smiles now, twenty-five years later, as she tells her story to our sharing group. "I just sailed past the arriving guests, saying I was off to AA and my husband would get them their drinks!" There she found people who would listen to her story, patiently, again and again, without judgment or advice-giving. They would support her in learning coping strategies, and offer insights only if asked for them.

sharing stories can heal

Sharing the stories of the disasters of alcohol abuse and the difficulty of recovery is at the heart of Alcoholics Anonymous and all the support groups for other problems it has inspired. To know that other people have walked the path we're on can be a great help.

There's an Asian tale about a woman who brings the sorrow over her son's death to the spiritual teacher. How can she possibly bear her grief? He gently suggests that she may find the answer by looking for a house in the village that has not been visited by death. The grieving woman searches door to door, in each place finding some story of sorrow, some lost love. She returns to the teacher still grieving, but healed of her deepest hurt because she knows she is not alone. Others have managed to live through what she is undergoing.[110]

I can see the relief on people's faces as I tell my own story of depression at seminars on bipolar illness. Other stories come forth from participants. The sense of isolation, the shame of feeling out of control, the loneliness of being "different" all soften when people realize their special kind of adversity is shared by others. Clues about ways to deal with this may come, yes; but the most important gift of such sharing is the sense of commonality. "I'm so relieved," said a participant at one seminar, "not to be the 'Lone Ranger' any more."

Sharing personal experiences, however, can slip easily into unsolicited advice. "I know just what you feel," is presumptuous at best. "I've been through the same thing and know just what to do" is worse. We can never presume to know what others are feeling until they tell us themselves. Empathy is not omniscience. While we may share the same problems, each of our responses is, in part, unique.

The key to companionship is compassionate inquiry: "Would you like me to share my own experience of dealing with this? Maybe something in it would strike a chord." Open-ended sharing, with no strings attached, is very different from sharing designed to make sure the sufferer takes our good advice. Unsolicited advice, however subtle, is likely to undercut compassionate connection.

However, never say *never*. Supporting others in suffering can't be run by a rule book. Depending on circumstances, people may need a firmer hand. At the depths of compassionate connection is attunement to the soul of this unique person who is here, now. Children who are frightened don't need, at first, a therapeutic airing of their inmost feelings, but firm reassurance: I'm here, and you'll be OK. In the first rush of anguish over severe disaster, the child in us may need just such firm reassurance, whatever our age.

A pastor I know who serves a largely immigrant Latino population is a master of such reassurance. Fortunately for their own emotional health, most of the members of his particular flock have not learned the "stiff upper lip" approach to the death of a loved one that so many Anglos still follow. When Fr. Dave arrives at the bedside of a recently deceased parishioner, "emotion is bouncing off the walls," with the loud cries and freely flowing tears of family members. "People let themselves fall apart for a while, all the more so when I, as the spiritual father, walk into the room." As the emotion subsides, and people begin saying that they "don't know what they're going to do," or that "they can't cope." Dave says that what's needed "is my most reassuring voice. 'First and foremost,' I tell them, 'you're going to get through this.' They nod. Father has said it, the child in them is calmed, and we can get down to adult planning."

The adult in us may also need real a firm hand at times. I got an unexpected but timely directive from Nancy, a spiritual friend, with whom I had gotten to sort out my continuing difficulties in trusting God fully. I had felt quite recently in prayer an invitation to "trust in the absolute goodness of God." Absolute goodness? In all circumstances? No matter what? Intellectually, I could consider the idea, but in my heart, old barriers to trust still ruled. As I poured out the all-too-familiar tale of all my difficulties in trusting, Nancy listened deeply, with great sympathy. "I do know about struggles like this, believe me," she responded. "What can I do?" I asked. She leaned toward me and replied in a strong, insistent whisper, "Get—over—it!"

I gasped as the unexpected words hit me with penetrating power. I let out a gasp. I must have been as shocked as poor Myrtle was, so many years before, when I told her to bless the pain in her legs instead of whining about it. "That simple, is it?" I asked. "For you, right now, yes," was the answer. "Trust is an action. You can't wait to unravel all the fears. Just do it. See what happens."

This shocking challenge helped me cross a threshold. I began practicing deeper trust. Such brusque advice at another time, or to another person, would have been unhelpful, counterproductive, or deeply hurtful. But Nancy had listened deeply enough to know that a challenge was called for. The Spirit spoke to me through her compassionate but bracing words.

The most important question to ask any time we are befriending a sufferer is, "What is called for—here, now?"[111] Real openness to the Spirit's guidance is our best guard against mistakes. And that takes prayer.

praying befriends the sufferer

Job's friends never pray with him or for him, while Job's own prayers for justice soar to God unsupported by those around him. "Prayerful support, and the presence of people prayerfully attuned, would have been helpful," says Sue about her post-firing struggle. Spiritually alone like Job, she finally turned to her own habitual resources: inspirational reading and meditation. After much struggle she came to "the place of accepting what I had brought to the situation and its unfolding. I was finally able to surrender, to say 'thy will be done' in, through, and in spite of all this." Knowing she was supported in prayer would have made things easier.

Such prayerful support led to a significant breakthrough between my friend Art and his son Miles. The teenage boy had begun to get into trouble when he entered high school, progressively challenging his parents' ability to deal with his behavior. "He's basically a good kid," Art declares, "but he's got some neurological disabilities we're still trying to understand, and he reacts badly to some situations."

The swim team was a particular trial for Miles, who took a dislike to the coach. In the new cyberspace style of America's teens, he posted his feelings on his own personal Web site. Unfortunately, his anger took the form of threatening words, just the wrong move in a day of increased vigilance against student violence. Suspended from school and threatened with criminal prosecution, Miles developed an even worse attitude, and the relationship with his parents became even more strained.

"This was a dark time for us," says Art. "Growing up as we did in very conservative social circumstances, teenage acting out meant a little harmless fun. We just didn't know how to deal with this. The utter shame of the events, especially having to sit in the principal's office several times and face the offended parties, was totally humiliating. I felt I could not share our problems with anyone nearby." Finally, Art found friends in Boston and poured it all out, haltingly, with many tears. "What a relief to ask someone for prayers!"

Later that day, "Miles was AWOL, on his bike, out somewhere—who knew where? I felt like someone lost at sea, starving and thirsty, desperate to do something, anything." Art remembered the friends praying for him. For the first time, it occurred to him that he could pray for his son. But what kind of prayer? Just thinking about Miles put his mind into confusion and his heart in turmoil. He idly reached for a devotional book he had been reading recently, and leafing through it found an imagistic prayer exercise about "caring for others in prayer" by bathing them in God's light.

As Art describes it, the light led him to a breakthrough with his son. "After becoming centered, I imagined my son very clearly, God's light enveloping him, enveloping me. I found that I was resisting the light strongly, holding my breath as if I were drowning. But the light was persistent, and I just gave in, taking a deep breath. The light took on a life of its own and surrounded Miles and me in a shimmering, supportive sphere. It was like discovering I could trust the ocean depths while scuba diving."

Out of the depths of the light came an image: the famous Russian icon of the Three Angels visiting Abraham—three beautiful, winged figures seated around the patriarch's table, symbolizing the threefold love of God as Creator, Redeemer, and Spirit. "Suddenly Miles and me were at the table surrounded by the light of God, welcoming both of us without judgment. I began to pray: 'Christ within you, Miles; Christ within me.'" As this prayer-dream unfolded, Miles became a small child carried up into the heavenly light, and Art was left alone, weeping anew, but this time with compassion, rather than grief. "I just had to let go of the whole situation, and it was OK," Art told me.

When Art finished praying, he discovered that Miles had come home, gotten upset, and had left again for parts unknown. Art, his helplessness set aside in the first stirrings of a new courage, set out on his own bike, prayed for guidance, and "against all reasonable odds found my son. Because the effects of the prayer were still with me, I could offer my company without judgmental words. We rode together to a distant park by the river, had a wonderful time, and were later welcomed by total strangers at a block party near the park." Hours later, exhausted but connected, father and son returned home. It was the beginning of the healing—and the beginning of a prayer for Miles his father has continued since then. Amazing grace, full and free, had come to them, flowing through the situation to salve its wounds and stir up healing energies.

When, like Art, or Sue's coworkers, we feel utterly at a loss for what to say or do, we can begin by praying. Whatever outer form our prayer takes, praying isn't just an exchange between God and our solitary souls. Because of the deep links of spirit that grow between people, and the interconnectedness of all our spirits in God, we are somehow present with the people for whom we pray, "present with the power of our Lord Jesus" as the apostle Paul tells the Corinthians, whether we are physically present with them or not.[112] When we pray for others we are all priests, mediators of grace.

In ways we cannot understand, but can experience, we can "present" others to God, just as we can present ourselves, and just as Christ presents the whole world to God in his great "high priestly prayer" in John 17. We are all in him and he is in us, and all of us, together, are in God. We can become the agents of God's presence to others. The physical touch of a hand, the audible word of comfort or challenge, or a truly listening silence can be strengthened by the silent power of inward prayer, which works in the secret depths of another's soul by the power of the Spirit.

At the very least, our prayers can help someone feel supported. But more important than that, prayer is a channel for the Spirit to inspire and strengthen people to deal with their challenges redemptively. Most importantly, we dare set no limit to the possibilities of goodness inherent in any situation that can be stirred into greater life through compassionate presence and loving prayer.

praying the world

HOW WE SUFFER MATTERS TO GOD. Our prayerful, conscious link to God's own courage in suffering is not for our sake alone, but for the sake of the world. Because suffering can lead to bitterness, resentment, and despair, it is one of the major breeding grounds for evil on the planet. From low-grade grumpiness over small inconveniences to the unconscious desire that others should share one's misery, from petty sniping to vengeful retaliation, suffering easily begets more suffering. In its crucible our very selves are shaped for good or ill. That is why it is so important for the narrowness of the suffering to be opened to the vastness of God's own courage, love, and life. Otherwise, suffering can easily become the devil's playground.

A young Israeli I met recently, whom I'll call Aaron, found himself in the midst of that sinister playground as a young man caught in the terrible, fratricidal strife of Jew against Arab and Arab against Jew in the Israeli–Palestinian struggle. Aaron had fallen into a deep friendship with an Arab boy he'd encountered at a youth camp for Arab-Jewish understanding, from whom he heard, for the first time, personal stories of Arab suffering. He already knew how the past sufferings of European Jews had led to the creation of a homeland for the Jewish people. He had never encountered, in the flesh, the difficulties Palestinian Arabs now faced under Jewish rule, especially in the occupied West Bank and Gaza. The evil of terrorist attacks against Israelis was clear to him; but now he had firsthand reports of actions that only fanned the flame of hatred, even as they sought to limit the terrorism. Both sides, out of their past victimhood, now victimized the other. Aaron decided he did not want to add to that suffering.

"When the time came for my army service, I determined that I would enter the army, but refuse to serve in the occupied territories," said Aaron to a group of us at a conference of Muslims, Christians, and Jews. He thus became one of the early "refuseniks." With its back against the sea, surrounded by Arab nations, the Israel Defense Force was in no mood for soldiers who refused to accept their assigned duties. Aaron soon found himself in military prison with its casual habit of mistreatment. He was kept in the large intake cell for many days with minimal food and sanitation as new prisoners came, were processed, and assigned to cell blocks. Only after calculated misbehavior got the attention of a less punitive officer was he processed for admission. Intimidation, threats, beatings, and isolation followed, all designed to nip this rebellion—one which has grown through the years among young Israelis—in the bud.

Matters came to a head one day when a crusty officer told him he would be handcuffed, hands to feet, and thrown in "with the rapists and murderers" if he did not comply. Though Aaron knew this brutal handcuff punishment could cause lifelong injuries, he stood by his commitment. The threat had been a last attempt to break him, and he was simply sent to the new wing. As it turned out, "the threatened wing was actually better, with smaller cells for two to four men, and showers, however dismal. I spent the rest of my imprisonment studying and preparing to continue my work," he told us.

Amazingly, while he still struggles with anger about his prison experiences, Aaron seems to bear no hatred against his native country. "I've moved from giving in to my anger to dealing with it. One response to suffering is humor," he says. "It creates a kind of perspective. Anger no longer determines my views." How did he manage to find humor while being so mistreated? "I explored the other options completely," he said with a wry smile, "and found that humor was much better." The humor, along with his determined courage, helped him find a space bigger than his suffering, where his commitment to human good could still grow. Released from prison and the army,

Aaron continued to work with other Jews and Arabs seeking a peaceful resolution of the conflict.

Aaron could easily have become just another embittered, hateful part of this heartbreaking conflict. But whether he consciously realized it or not, he was cooperating with the streams of divine grace that constantly flow through the world, inviting us to join God in creating good. Though he was not a religious Jew, his courage helped him find, beginning with humor, the larger space where good can flourish, where resurrection begins. This has, in turn, led to a search for what Judaism has to say about the God who is the true source of the larger soul-space he has begun to discover.

In just such silent but solid ways, God companions us in suffering to make it an occasion for redemption. Wherever a sufferer finds the courage to choose life not death, to bless rather than curse, the power of resurrection shines. This is why Christian tradition believes that, in and through Christ's way of dealing with suffering, even on the cross, "God is reigning from the Tree,"[113] as an ancient Good Friday hymn puts it. In himself, he has triumphed over the dark inner forces that would drag him into becoming a perpetrator of suffering. By taprooting his life into God's goodness he was able to endure the darkness of abandonment, forgive his enemies, and trust the eternally springing life of God's love to sustain him. By so doing, Christ was able to manifest the power of resurrection that springs from the heart of God's own life.[114]

This Christ is more than a man who lived two thousand years ago as an example, more even than an Incarnation that took place at a specific time. Christ is the revelation of the way God works, always and everywhere, to incorporate our entire lives, suffering and all, into the divine life itself. Wherever this Christ-like pattern takes hold in a life, suffering can become the occasion for good, and new life can spring forth in the midst of death-dealing powers.

the testing power of adversity

Because we live in a soul-shaping universe, the way we suffer either helps or hinders the progress of God's gracious purposes.

That is why the Bible sees adversity as the occasion for the "trial" or "testing" of our mettle, as mentioned in Chapter One.

Testing is not some arbitrary game played by a distant God, toying with us to see if we will be obedient. It is a condition of life itself, built into the very fabric of the universe. Life contains challenges to be met as well as delights to be savored. Sooner or later, the baby has to face the test of whether it can stand on its feet yet and walk. The patience of parents is tested by the baby's successful toddling. Good testing in schools invites pupils to flex the muscles of their knowledge. Athletes set tests for themselves to stretch their abilities and discover where they need improvement. When we test metals to find where flaws may be hidden, the purpose is to craft stronger metal, not to condemn or criticize.

Just so, circumstances, by their very nature, test us. While God may cross our path with a specific challenge at times, the Spirit can use any adversity, whatever the cause, to "seek the ground" of our heart, revealing us to ourselves, and compassionately strengthening us.[115]

Most of these tests come in forms much less dramatic than Aaron's bold resistance to authority. Take Juli and the food pantry, for example. As she became increasingly aware of homelessness near her affluent suburb, Juli felt called by God to involve her own parish in staffing a food pantry in a nearby town. With her time already overcommitted, "it was my strong wish not to be in charge of the project," she says, "but to challenge my church to look beyond its comfortable surroundings." People agreed it was a real need, and some volunteered to help, but no one stepped forward to organize the effort. Finally, "after many attempts to get out of running it, I did end up in charge for several years," Juli muses. Her commitment to following God's call was tested by the disinclination of her fellow parishioners to be the leaders, and found true by her willingness to take charge and train leaders to succeed her.

Every challenge we face can become a deeper initiation into the pattern and power of resurrection life. My friend Art's love for his son, as we saw in Chapter Eight, was sorely tested by his son's behavior. But the trial he faced when a new minister changed his church's worship style was just as important, even though Art sees it as "minor and personal." Disagreements over church matters can be as great a hindrance to God's purposes as military brutality—sometimes worse.

After years of spiritual nurture in a formal, high-church Episcopal setting, Art resented the new "mega-church style, crafted to entertain." In spite of his efforts to adjust, Art found himself in real turmoil, bereft of the familiar worship that supported his prayer. Loss turned into resentment, and resentment into resistance to church attendance, which became "a pain I chose, with increasing frequency, to avoid." A former parish leader, Art was drifting away, undermining the strong pattern of his family's commitment to the church.

His practice of personal centering prayer and *lectio divina*—devotional reading of Scripture—continued. One summer morning, his attention was captured by the words Jesus hears at his baptism: "You are my Son, my beloved; my favor rests on you!"[116] "As the meditation continued, I saw a radiance over Christ's head. I began to 'hear' God say to me, 'You are my son, my beloved.' Then I started hearing God say it to my own children, and to my wife, and to other people. The radiance hovered over them, too."

Resentfully enduring the worship service next Sunday, Art was startled to "hear," inwardly, God saying, "You are my Son, my beloved; my favor rests on you," to the minister. Tears came to Art's eyes. "Suddenly this man was God's son, just trying to serve God in the way he thinks best. That mattered much more than whether I liked this worship style or not." As his heart filled with the sense of God's sheer favor toward human beings, his inner eye could see the radiance hovering over everyone in the church. "Maybe I'm weird, but I really needed something concrete like the imagined radiance." The image has become an enduring gift. Art recalls the radiance and thinks, "You are God's beloved," often, "especially in tense situations or when I'm finding it difficult to like the person I'm speaking to. It helps me let others be who they really are."

There have been worse outcomes to church conflicts. Art chose to stop being a passive victim of liturgical change and start practicing redemption. Sorely tried, he chose not to let dissatisfaction stand in the way of the enlargement of his heart. His small prayer was caught up into God's own life, and his spirit was raised from this small death to larger life.

God's own risk in an unfinished universe

We may not know all the reasons for suffering, but our lives are, in part, the discovery of its uses. Since the mystery of the suffering world is, ultimately, the mystery of the suffering Christ, its most important use is to open our hearts to the flow of God's own lament over the destructiveness of human folly, longing for human cooperation, and laboring to reshape the human heart in the divine image.

Choices as "minor and personal" as Art's are part of the ongoing formation of the world, for the world is far from complete. Between the good creation and its even better goal, God has undertaken the risky adventure of developing creation in cooperation with creatures free to make choices that can result in either good or evil.

What God "finishes" at the original creation, as discussed in Chapter One, is the good foundation, manifest in the world's building blocks—the elements, structural patterns like gravity, the gene code that flowers in millions of creatures, and the fundamental instincts of those creatures, including human beings. These are all good. Very good. But they are just raw materials, needing further development.

After the Creator's commanding voice binds the primal powers of chaos into these good foundations, God sets the materials free to develop, as we discussed in Chapter Two. A certain degree of chaos remains a real force, both creative and destructive, in the world. To blame God for this, as if it could be otherwise, is to misunderstand the fabric of reality. This world, as Job discovered, is much wilder than we imagine it to be. From angels to anchovies, all creatures have the power to behave in unpredictable and often colliding ways. As biology has demonstrated in the past 150 years, accident and randomness in the natural world are inevitable parts of the development of life on this planet. The biblical saga actually anticipates this scientific realization in its so-called "primitive" portrayal of God's struggle with the forces of chaos, not only in the primal creation, but recurrently. Biblically speaking, God's response to chaos is a prime factor in creation and redemption.[117]

In the midst of the destructive aspects of this wildness, continuing creation and redemption weave a golden thread. All creatures participate in shaping the still-emerging world: Beavers build dams and divert streams; plants cross-pollinate, producing variants. Free will is one of these raw materials. Our very nature demands that we choose between conflicting urges and desired outcomes. Human beings live in a world of firm foundations and perilous, tumultuous freedom.

We may have no say in the set of urges given us, and little control over which opportunities come our way, but we have real power to shape how we respond, and to let how we respond be shaped by the grace of God. Since we are able to choose ignorance, foolishness, and even mean-spiritedness, the very goodness of the universe itself makes moral evil possible. Sentient creatures could not exist otherwise; divine control of human freedom would be destructive to our existence, even though our choices can lead to great tragedies.

Such a universe is, therefore, in constant need of what the Jewish mystical tradition calls *tikkun ha'olam*—"repair" or redemption. Jesus insists that "My Father is working still" for that repair, not resting.[118] God's *redemptive* goodness is manifested by the Spirit's work "in all things" to weave patterns of good even in the midst of evil. As the Jesuit poet Gerard Manley Hopkins puts it, in spite of the "smear" of sin and evil,

> *. . . the Holy Ghost over the bent*
> *World broods with warm breast, and with, ah, bright wings.*[119]

Each of our choices, especially how we respond to adversity, either draws us deeper into that good "brooding" of the Spirit or closes us off from it. God yearns to draw our lives completely into delight at the world's goodness, and desires to redeem and repair its wounds. The promise of the gospel is that God will not stop working until the whole universe flowers into "the kingdom," where "righteousness and peace will kiss each other," justice will "roll down like waters," and the earth will be saturated with an intimate, knowing participation in God's love "as the waters cover the sea."[120]

The Spirit invites, supports, and cooperates with the even slightest human inclination toward truth, justice, healing, and love. As we "groan inwardly," tested by the challenges we face, these feelings can be offered to become part of the slow "manifestation of the children of God," those "fellow workers"[121] who can be the true stewards of life on earth, lending all their energies to the manifestation of the energies of the kingdom, sharing with God the task of facing evil redemptively, not destructively.[122] So Juli's staffing the food pantry, and Art's returning to church, and Aaron's enduring suffering without succumbing to hatred all cooperate with the God who seeks the best possible outcomes even in the worst of circumstances.

the world needs to be prayed

The world with all its pleasures and pains isn't simply meant to be experienced, still less to be worried about. This world is meant to be *prayed,* to find voice through us. Every encounter with goodness is a call to praise, every brush with suffering a call to prayer, a participation in the world's own yearning for God. Every challenge we face is an invitation to enter more deeply into the pattern and power of the always-available divine Life manifested in Christ. Our praise participates in God's own joy, our petitions in God's own caring, our bravery in God's own courage. Gradually, by the grace of this participation, we become "partakers of the divine nature," according to the writer of 2 Peter, sharing in God's ongoing own creative and redemptive activity.[123]

God is fitting us, here and hereafter, for our share in that work. All those who suffer courageously and compassionately are being drawn more deeply into participation in God's own life. When we join our personal sufferings to Christ's way of suffering, our capacity for compassion not only grows, but opens us to the great Compassion that companions our lives.

I saw this powerfully one day, during a visit with a friend to the memorial to AIDS victims at the Cathedral of St. John the Divine in New York City. Hundreds of memorial candles burned at the shrine, each a poignant prayer for a loved one. The sadness of lives lost hung in the air. As we turned to leave, my eye was captured by a huge wooden crucifix standing near the cathedral entrance. I had passed it by without particular interest when entering the cathedral, but now, filled with the resonance of this suffering, I saw the figure on it in a different light. The body of the crucified Man was strong, muscular, massive in its power. Its wounds, deep and hurtful as they might be, were small in comparison with the strength and vitality of that body, which radiated from deep within an enormous life. As I gazed upwards at the compassionate eyes, I felt how much our small lives are carried in a great, strong Life that can bear with, bear up under, and finally bear away those wounds, healing them from within, just as the body's natural grace heals its wounds. We are carried in the life of a God who bears our wounds with us, working with us, through us, to bring healing through the very wounds themselves.

when we pray, we act

Humanity, as part of the very structure of the world, has been given a prime place in the mediation of God's grace to the world. A great deal of piety recoils at the very thought. How can mere humans imagine that God depends on our praying? Yet it seems quite natural to think that when serving the poor, tending the sick, and otherwise meeting physical needs, humans share God's work. Why not when we pray? When we hold people and situations in God's light, are we allowing grace to work in a situation more fully than it might otherwise be able to? The Scriptures are quite clear: "[E]ffectual fervent prayer . . . avails much," according to James, the Lord's own brother.[124] Jesus himself makes it clear that when two or three of us pray in accord, it makes a difference in the life of the world.[125]

Because God will not violate human freedom, a certain measure of human willingness is needed for the Spirit to move freely in the human family. Through prayer God gives us a share in the Spirit's work. The effect of opening our own spirits to grace does not stop at the borders of our psyche, but can radiate out toward others.

Indeed, human intention, including fervent prayer (the deepest form of human intention) is the missing element in the modern scientific picture of the world. It is true that our modern scientific knowledge about the implacable, impersonal mechanisms of nature gives us good reason to disagree with our ancestors who saw all natural disaster as punishment for sin. Jesus himself questions this blanket assumption, making room for accident as a reality in God's world, when he says, "[T]hose eighteen who were killed when the tower of Siloam fell on them—do you think that they were worse offenders than all the others living in Jerusalem?"[126] Sincere prayer will not stop tidal waves, for example, once an earthquake has aroused them. So much is true.

But much of the mayhem that affects human life is not the result of such implacable forces, and, as we have noted, more than one natural disaster has been abetted by humanity's own destructive behavior. Prayer *evokes possibilities* in situations that might otherwise remain latent, and is intended by God to be a vital ingredient in shaping the outcomes of all of events, no matter the cause.

Many years ago, while making a long trip, I fell into a reverie about the looming worldwide environmental crisis. After a period of stewing emotionally and feeling helpless about the pollution of the waters, the poisoning of the rain, and the steady invasion of the rain forests, I began to feel a prayer welling up spontaneously from deep within me. A set of seemingly incoherent sounds and feelings at first, it slowly shaped itself into a series of "calls" for leaders small and great to emerge, raised up by the Spirit to help humanity in this crisis. Far from a pleading *to* God to do something, it felt like a prayer *from* God, through me, to the soul of the world. As Paul says in Romans, deep prayer is always the Spirit praying through us.

That prayer has been with me since, like an underground stream, occasionally breaking into consciousness. I dare to believe that my small stream of prayer is part of the Spirit's larger river of passionate love moving through the hearts of countless other human beings, inviting the good to flourish. Every human being is called to be part of the "God saves the world" project, and this is one aspect of my part.

It's hard to tell, just looking at the headlines, that this Spirit-driven prayer has been fruitful, but from time to time I believe I see a sign. I was recently moved to tears by a TV news story about a high school senior from California who won a National Science Prize for inventing an ocean buoy that, simply by rocking back and forth in the waves, generates electrical power. Growing up with an awareness of our fossil fuel and global warming dilemma, this bright young man decided we "need all the good ideas we can get," and set to work on one. Something in me whispered, "*This* is how God saves the world."

We live in apocalyptic times. I do not think, as all too many Christians seem to, that the world is about to end. But it is clear that humanity faces some of its greatest challenges in the coming century, including the very real possibility of enormous suffering through environmental crisis, war over resources, and the distresses of overpopulation. In the light of this, learning to face our own adversities courageously, to be compassionate supporters of others in their difficulties, and to take our part in praying the world are key to accepting God's own invitation to share in the work of world-healing and re-creation.

Realizing the challenge our species faces is a call to bravery, not fruitless fretting. The playwright and poet Christopher Fry even calls us to be thankful for trying times:

Thank God our time is now when wrong
Comes up to face us till we take
The longest stride of soul men ever took. . . .[127]

A long stride of soul is what's called for if we are to join God's own mission of redemptive love to this suffering, still-evolving world, which yearns to be ruled by human beings truly aligned with God's loving purposes. God is not finished yet, either with the world or with humanity.

Each small adversity we face with courage can make us more able to stand with others, and help them grow in grace through their own difficulties. When we stand prayerfully with others in their trials, God strengthens, through the open channels of our hearts, the web of grace that surrounds those in need. Often we have no idea of the effects of our prayers. Sometimes what happens seems startling.

The morning of the World Trade Center disaster, my friend Daniel learned the news from a friend. He turned on the radio, heard of the Pentagon attack, and knew this was not some fluke accident, but a real terrorist attack. "My immediate response was to think, 'Thank God it's over,' but then the awful realization came that there could be yet another plane headed for yet another target."

Daniel says that a "deep moan of prayer" reached from deep within him out to that fourth, possible plane. He stopped working and ran the eight blocks to church to his usual sanctuary of prayer in the chapel, where he lay prostrate in front of the altar. "As I ran," he relates, "a specific prayer formed: If there is another plane, may the passengers fight!" He lay in the darkness of the chapel in urgent prayer. "I was somehow standing with them as they faced their ordeal." After forty-five minutes or so, the urgency passed. He didn't yet know the fourth plane had crashed, saved from causing further destruction by the actions of the passengers.

I don't imagine, nor does Daniel, that his prayer, however urgent, directly caused what happened. But I do believe that his prayer was one strand, along with thousands of others, in the web of grace the Spirit was weaving around those passengers. Daniel's prayer was part of his sharing in God's desires for the world. His compassionate concern connected him to the fellowship of all who face their own suffering redemptively, and help others to do so. This is what Christians call the "communion of saints"—the fellowship of all the brave and loving, both the ones on earth and those in a greater light whose ongoing prayer, born out of their participation in the groanings and growing of creation, is part of the world's weaving.[128]

join the company of all who live redemptively

In my mid-twenties, during prayer I had a powerful inner image of this fellowship of all who live redemptively in the spirit of Christ. This image has given meaning to my prayers and actions ever since. I was standing in an ancient room like the Sistine Chapel in Rome. On the wall was a giant fresco like Michelangelo's *Last Judgment,* with its startling blue background, but the Christ in the mural was totally different. Instead of descending from above, hand sweeping down to consign the wicked to hell, he stood as if on a mountaintop, hand raised and eyes turned toward a great Light that fell from above, his face radiating triumph after long struggle. His other strong hand reached down to clasp the hand of a man in the last stages of scaling the summit. That man, in turn, reached down to a woman climbing over an obstacle. Her left hand held the hand of the person below her.

The emerging image gradually revealed the entire mountain, which rose out of darkness into light. On its slopes thousands of people helped each other to the next step of the ascent. The people near the top were stronger, more fully muscled than those below. The strugglers at the bottom were often dazed or confused, not quite sure how to proceed in the twilight hovering above the dark shadows from which they had emerged. But the enormous strength of the figure at the summit flowed down through all those linked hands and straining muscles to nourish their hearts and vitalize their bodies, drawing them upward with magnetic power.

The whole mountain of people was united in one movement of world-redeeming grace.

That vision has haunted, inspired, and called me every step of the way, in black holes and out of them, in the face of immovable rocks and removable obstacles, through depressions and anxieties. I sometimes remember it when some petty annoyance has knocked me off the path of patience, or personal difficulty has blocked the flow of compassion. For me it is a symbol of how we love and pray one another into fuller communion with God's generous and victorious love, which will not stop, no matter how long it takes, until it shapes us fully into a reflection of its own strong and compassionate beauty.[129]

If that is true, and I believe it is, each act of suffering redemptively is but the next step on a great journey into God, which we have only just begun.

For help in discerning how God is working for good in your life, see Prayer Exercise 6 in the Appendix.

a greeting to the risen one

When You rose, hallowed, harrowed One,
it was not without your scars
You come as one who has known hell;
You carry the memory deep within your eyes
and see it everywhere it lurks.

Let the trumpets be at least a little muted
in recognition that this victory is never won
without passages too difficult even to speak of
in the light of day.

Yet You come as one who knows also,
beyond the deepest reaches of any hell,
that mothering Dark
out of which all Light is born,
and you carry that, too,
in the sinewy lightness of your Gaze.[130]

APPENDIX

*prayer exercises
for facing suffering
redemptively*

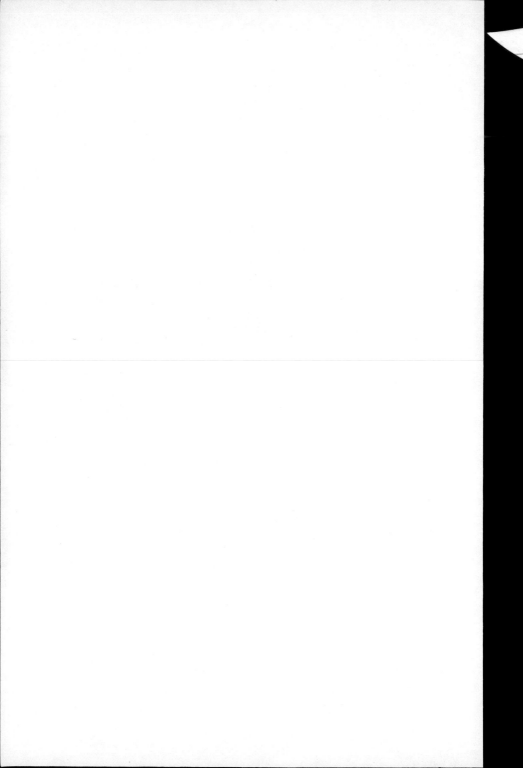

INTRODUCTION

PRAYER IS A NATURAL CAPACITY of every human being. Like the ability to sing or talk, our ability to pray grows with practice. That we need to learn skills to relate to the Spirit should not surprise us, since increasing skill—in communicating, loving, understanding, changing—is required to deepen any relationship we have.

The following prayer exercises are, therefore, precisely that—*exercises* for soul and spirit the same way we do exercises for the body, and learn to exercise patience, compassion, or even charm in human relationships.

The exercises given are designed to relate to the text of the book. Many of them are referred to in anecdotes about how people pray their way through suffering, and are offered in the hope that they may be of help to anyone facing a challenge to avail themselves more deeply of the "grace to help in time of need" so freely offered by God. They are meant to supplement, not replace, whatever forms of prayer are already fruitful.

These meditative prayer forms invite an openness to the inner life seldom encouraged in our culture, even in our religious devotion, but deeply rooted in Christian prayer practice. The reader is encouraged to be truly open to images, words, or feelings that may arise in prayer. On occasion, startling, unfamiliar, or unpleasant images may come unbidden. This is not to be feared, since our inner lives contain much. The spiritual rule of thumb in dealing with images is this: Let yourself go with images that seem good and true according to your understanding of God, and decline, for the moment, images that are doubtful or upsetting. Simply note them, and let them go.

This does not mean every new or startling image is wrong. But it does mean one needs to take time to discern whether this image is a distraction, or the introduction, by the Spirit, of some deeper truth about God or the self that may be within a Christian heritage, but unknown to the person who prays. I have come to trust that if we truly intend to be open to God in prayer, we need not be afraid of what comes to us, even if we may decide, after due consideration, that it is the product of our own mind, or a even disturbance not to be trusted.

These exercises, therefore, are meant to be used as part of a growing spiritual practice that includes study, worship, and fellowship with others on the path. Any deeper form of prayer is best practiced with the spiritual guidance of a seasoned group or spiritual director.

PRAYER EXERCISE ONE

breathing into the spaciousness of God

This prayer exercise can increase your sense of living, moving, and having your being in the boundless space of God's life and grace—the "midnight sky" referred to in Chapter One. Practiced in solitude, it can become habitual enough to accompany you anywhere.

1. *Make an intention* to let yourself become aware of the reality that your life is, always and everywhere, "in God."

2. *Begin by following your breath*—that is, focusing your full consciousness on the simple act of breathing, from beginning to end: the breathing in; the infilling, felt in your torso; and the letting-go or exhaling. Follow each breath appreciatively, becoming aware of the unnoticed miracle of how our little breath belongs to the God-given oceanic breath of life that surrounds the whole planet. If distractions keep pulling you away from breath-awareness, use a prayer phrase like *breathing God within me* or *breathing life within me* to focus your attention.

3. *Imagine the vastness of the night sky,* or, if you prefer, an open daytime expanse where you can see all the way to the horizon. Let yourself feel the expanse, the spaciousness, the great arc of the sky embracing the earth.

4. *Focus your attention on the air immediately around you,* and realize (or imagine) how you are breathing in this small portion of the vast ocean. After a while, expand your focus further to the immediate area beyond the room or space you're in. Then expand it to the whole area surrounding that.

Finally, imagine that your breathing can reach all the way to the horizon, bringing in God's life-giving air from this vast area. Have a sense of the dome of the sky above you and the firmness of the earth beneath you. Imagine what is, in fact, the truth: that this air is alive with the life of God, and that the invisible life of God surrounds and fills you like this air. Affirm and claim in faith that you are living, moving, and breathing in a life far vaster than your own. Remember that you are always surrounded by this vastness, which reaches in its embrace all the way to the air around your body, a powerful symbol of God's own vastness and nearness.

6. *Gradually withdraw your focus* from the far horizon, stage by stage, back to your own body. Finish with a prayer of thanks that, always and everywhere, you live in the boundless space of God's grace.

PRAYER EXERCISE TWO

a form of centering prayer: being present to God

Forms of contemplative prayer vary, but most use the method of simple focus to cleanse the mind and heart of distracting thoughts and open the self to the Spirit, being simply present to God, presenting whatever arises to the divine mercy and grace.

1. *Prepare the body to be quiet and receptive,* in any posture that will help you stay alert: sitting upright, kneeling with support, or standing. You may find that hands folded encourages stillness, palms unfolded and upturned invites openness, and arms wide and raised gives rise to praise.

2. *Slowly repeat a breath-prayer* or a chosen prayer phrase of only a few words as a "dart of love" toward the mystery of God. This phrase, gently repeated, has the power to gather your attention gradually into a calm, alert, receptive focus on one thing only. As distractions arise, passively disregard them, letting them come and go. When you notice the mind following an outside noise or an inner thought, gently disengage, without self-blame, and return to the phrase. You can either coordinate the prayer phrase with your breathing, or simply focus on the phrase itself, with intention. The name of Jesus, or the Jesus Prayer ("Lord Jesus Christ, Son of the living God, have mercy on me, a sinner") are traditional prayer phrases, but feel free to find a phrase that turns your heart and mind toward God.

3. *Let the phrase go* when you sense that your consciousness is focused without undue distraction, and let your focused consciousness be filled with a simple intention to be open to the invisible God who is present in you and around you—still, open, receptive, without any specific expectation, other than availability to God. If distractions crowd in, return for a while to the prayer phrase to refocus your attention.

4. *Alternatively,* you can choose an attribute of God, such as love, or courage, or compassion, and fill your heart and mind with a remembrance of that quality. You might use an inwardly held image of this attribute. Or you can present whatever arises— thoughts, feelings, aches, pains—to God. Note each one and let them go into God's love.

5. *Conclude with a simple, from the heart, sentence of prayer*—either spontaneously, out of your experience, or a favorite memorized prayer.

PRAYER EXERCISE THREE

finding personal meaning
in biblical stories

To create a personal profile of how ordinary stories, sacred stories, and biblical stories help frame your life, spend time journaling some answers to the following questions.

1. *Name one of your favorite childhood storybook tales.* As you remember the story, what values does it embody? What aspect of the human soul does it emphasize? How have these values become part of your ongoing life—moral landmarks by which you orient yourself?

2. *What's one of your favorite Bible stories?* Retell it to yourself. What values does it embody? What aspect of the human soul does it emphasize? What aspects of the nature and presence of God does it emphasize?

3. *Compare and contrast the two tales.* Do the similarities and differences between the values in the tales reflect change or continuity? How do the stories reinforce or fight against each other? If they are in conflict, ponder and pray about clarifying your values.

4. *Choose a Bible Story* that intrigues or bothers you—or one that seems particularly appropriate to your situation. Read it

through, looking for values, virtues, or attributes of both God and human beings. That is, what aspects of God are at work in the story—creator, parent, judge, challenger, friend, lover, warrior? What aspects of human nature are drawn out in the tale? How do these elements affect you as you read the story? What "powers" do you see at work in this biblical tale? How do you see these elements of human nature and spiritual powers at work in your world?

5. *Summarize your reflections in a sentence or two.* It's helpful to play with sentence completion, beginning with a set phrase like, *"This indicates that I am a person who*_____. *God's presence in this story is like*_____.*"*

Let these sentences become a meditative prayer by repeating slowly, in harmony with your breath, *"I am* _____; *Thou art* _____.*"*

PRAYER EXERCISE FOUR
presenting yourself and others to God

This prayer includes, in a contemplative, meditative style, the two common types of petition, or asking, and intercession, or "going in between" God and another person, asking a blessing for that person.

1. *Begin by practicing* the first three steps of Centering Prayer in order to focus your attention on and open your heart to God. Or use the first two steps of Prayer Exercise One, "Breathing into the Spaciousness."

2. *Coming to the moment of simple intention* to be available to God, let whatever is in you, whatever you choose to present, be held in your awareness and offered, opened to the Spirit. If it is a pain in your body, or an emotional hurt, let it be in that presence, affirmed in faith. If it is a delight or a remembered blessing, offer it in gratitude. You may affirm God's presence by imagining it as a radiant, shimmering light surrounding and permeating you, or

as the secret aliveness within, beyond the ocean of air that envelops you. Let what you offer simply be present, bathed, or suffused in a sense of that presence.

3. *You may choose to give voice* to your pain or delight in words, or sounds, or even body movements—but keep your attention on the surrounding presence into which you are offering yourself. You may also choose to let this prayer become conversational, pouring out your heart to God. But be sure to keep the sense of offering these words, and the feelings within them, into the larger space of God within you and around you, rather than making the words the center of your attention.

4. *Give thanks,* now, before any tangible results of your praying emerge. Trust that the energy of your prayers can be taken by the Spirit of God and woven into God's own mission of creation, repair, and redemption.

5. *Use this prayer for others* by imagining that you are speaking on their behalf, or holding them, problems and all, into the light of God. Just let them *be* there, absorbing God's goodness, to do in them and through them the highest good God intends for them, whatever that may be.

PRAYER EXERCISE FIVE

investing in the treasury of the heart

The first part of this prayer exercise is based on the ancient Eastern Orthodox "hesychast" practice of focusing on the heart area, "putting the mind in the heart" as some Eastern teachers advise. The second part puts into practical use Jesus' metaphor of the "treasure of the heart."

1. *Begin by practicing* the first step of Centering Prayer in order to focus your attention on the divine presence.

2. *Shift the focus* to the symbolic heart area, deep in the middle of the chest, as you begin your short prayer phrase. You may also

choose to symbolize the Spirit's presence in the heart by imagining a gently glowing light in the heart area.

3. *Begin remembering moments of goodness and grace.* Savor them slowly, one by one, without rushing. Use all your senses— seeing, touching, hearing, smelling, body sense—to recapture the moment as vividly as possible. Marinate yourself in this goodness, with a sense of appreciation, gratitude, and thanksgiving.

4. *Vary your prayer phrase,* if you wish, to fit the memory. More important than words, however, *let the good feelings* of delight, or joy, or appreciation flow.

5. *Conclude with a brief verbal prayer:* The opening verses of Psalm 103, for example, provide many phrases that, if memorized, can give voice to your thanksgiving: *Bless the LORD, O my soul . . . all that is within me, bless his holy name . . . do not forget all his benefits —who forgives all your iniquity, who heals all your diseases . . . redeems your life . . . crowns you with steadfast love and mercy . . . satisfies you with good as long as you live so that your youth is renewed like the eagle's. Vindication and justice for all who are oppressed.* [131]

PRAYER EXERCISE SIX
God works with us for good

As Scripture tells us, "God works together with those who love him to bring about what is good," or, "In all things God works for good." Christian faith affirms that no situation is beyond redemption; no matter how small or great, it can be woven, by the Spirit's work, into a larger pattern of good, so that "neither life nor death nor any power under heaven can separate us from the love of God which is in Christ Jesus our Lord." This exercise is a good way to "call to mind the deeds of the Lord" (Psalm 77:11).

1. *Remember* a few difficult times that have occurred in your life. In each case, "reinhabit" that time using all your powers of memory.

2. *Write down* the ways in which each case challenged you: Was it a challenge to your fear, to your faith, to love in a relationship, to your confidence in yourself? Write down also some of the ways you coped with that situation.

3. *As you remember with gratitude* how you survived and coped, open your mind and heart prayerfully, and ask the Spirit to show you some good that has come out of this situation that you may not have seen before.

4. *Ask the Spirit* to show you, also, how God may have been present in ways you did not realize at the time. Be open to what comes, through feelings, or inner images, or ideas.

5. *Write your reflections* in a spirit of thanksgiving, or as an actual prayer.

6. *Repeat this exercise* for other difficult moments to keep building up your sense of how God has worked with you to bring good out of adversity.

7. *Use this exercise for some current difficulty* you are having, looking especially at a) grace that is available in ways you may not have realized; b) good that may already have come out of this situation; c) ways in which God is present—to your soul inwardly, through other people, through nature, or through circumstances.

ACKNOWLEDGMENTS

NO BOOK IS BORN IN SOLITUDE. Its birth is a mysterious combination of seed-ideas that have come from the many lives the writer has listened to. Just so, everything I have written would not have been possible without mentors and teachers, friends and colleagues, parishioners and students who have shared their ideas, reflections, stories, laughter, tears, doubts, faith, and encounters with God.

To mention some is to leave others out, but for this work on suffering I am especially indebted to Thayer Green, my sometime therapist and spiritual mentor, who first taught me many years ago to "befriend" my own soul, and Frederick Shriver, my seminary tutor and lifelong friend, both of whom shared my journey toward wholeness, and their own wisdom about how to walk the path of this wondrous, difficult, and richly graced world. My wife, soul mate, and companion of over three decades, Suzanne, has also brought her laughter and healing touch to many dark hours, and has taught me time and again that appreciation is the beginning of wisdom.

As the text of this book demonstrates, the stories of other people—many of whose names and circumstances have been slightly altered to protect their privacy—have companioned and guided my own emerging thoughts. But I can openly name those who graciously consented to form a circle of readers for the draft of this book: Dr. David Bate, Jean Clain, Jr., Fr. John Cockayne, Bob and Bobbie Festa, Tom Holt, Carolyn Klinger-Keiter, Kay Locke, Lori McConnell, Puran Lucas Perez, Jane Riedel, Juli Towell, Mark Waldon, and Sue Zivi. Their comments, critique, and reassurance were invaluable. Through people like all of these, I have come to know, more deeply, that God's promise to be with us involves the gift of companions on the journey.

January 1, 2005
South Orange, New Jersey

NOTES

1 Medical research has demonstrated that bipolar or manic-depression is, in part, a physical disease—the result of genetic factors reinforced or evoked by social environment. Treatment includes medication and some form of psychotherapy. Medication is often necessary for the duration of the patient's lifetime to control the mood swings. With proper medical treatment, a bipolar depressive may safely and effectively use various complementary therapies, including spiritual practice. For further information see Mary Ellen Copeland, *The Depression Workbook* (Oakland, CA: New Harbinger, 1992), *Living Without Depression and Manic Depression* (Oakland, CA: New Harbinger, 1992).

2 The "Test" is a major motif in both Testaments, describing the way God works in situations of adversity, whatever their cause, to bring forth our true character, refining the image of God in us. Abraham is tested, as is Israel in the desert and Christ in the wilderness. For further discussion, see Chapter Eight.

3 For a spiritually rooted moral philosophy based on the reality of life's difficulty, see Scott Peck, *The Road Less Traveled* (New York: Touchstone, 2nd ed., 1998), p. 15.

4 See a fuller discussion of this spiritual practice of blessing in Robert Corin Morris, *Wrestling with Grace: A Spirituality for the Rough Edges of Daily Life* (Nashville: Upper Room, 2003), especially chapter 1, "The Second Breath."

5 1 Kings 18:28.

6 The popularity of this "scapegoat" version of the Passion is amply demonstrated by the huge response to Mel Gibson's 2004 film *The Passion of the Christ,* with its adorative attention to the physical pains of Christ. This theological approach is more deeply rooted in Western Christianity than in Eastern Orthodoxy, and is only

one among many "theories" of the Atonement. Many scholars feel the major biblical emphasis on atonement is otherwise. The warrior, or "Christus Victor" model of understanding the Atonement, was a major mode of interpretation in the Church of the first five centuries; this model is discussed in greater depth in Chapter Two.

7 Psalm 22:9.

8 Psalm 145:8.

9 Rollo May, *The Courage to Create* (New York: Norton and Co., 1994), p. 13.

10 See the story of the Flood in Genesis 6:1–8, of God's anger at Israel in Exodus 32:9–13, and the apparent breaking of the covenant in Psalm 89 for examples of this divinely vivid, emotional life.

11 Origen of Alexandria, *Contra Celsum* 51-52; Philip Schaff, *Early Church Fathers* (Peabody, MA: Henrickson Publishing, 1985). Available on the World Wide Web from Christian Classics Etherial Library at: http://www.ccel.org/fathers/ANF-04/Origen/12/t101.htm

12 Romans 15:4.

13 Ephesians 4:15.

14 Romans 12:21.

15 See Isaiah 63:9 (KJV).

16 See Proverbs 8:30 and Job 38:4–7 for these supplementary accounts of the Creation. The Scriptures actually tell four different but interrelated creation tales—the Word and Wind that call forth all things from the dark watery chaos (Genesis 1); the potter God who molds the human from the dust of the earth and lets the human name all the creatures (Genesis 2); the Architect and his masterworkers, who together "laid the foundations of the world" in Proverbs 8 and Job 38; and the even more ancient tale of the Warrior-Creator who slays the Sea Monster and triumphs over the vast abyss of chaos (alluded to in Psalm 74 and 89). The last is a story told all over the ancient Middle East in many cultures. Each provides a clue to the patterns of God's creative activities.

17 See Genesis 1:26, which emphasizes the divine image, with power to care for creation, and 2:7, which emphasizes our roots in the soil. The Hebrew *adam* is from *adamah*, dusty red earth; hence, "earthling" is a good translation.

18 See Genesis 6:5–12, especially in Everett Fox, *The Five Books of Moses* (New York: Schocken, 1997).

19 See Genesis 6:6 (NRSV and Fox).

20 See Genesis 6:8.

21 See the fascinating discussion of this in Marvin Pope, *The Anchor Bible: The Song of Songs*, (Garden City, New York: Doubleday, 1977).

22 See Song of Songs 8:6-7.

23 Song of Songs 6:10.

24 See Isaiah 50:1.

25 Hosea 11:8, 2:14, 15b.

26 Micah 6:8.

27 Exodus 15:3.

28 See Psalm 10:9–10.

29 Psalm 59:4, 35:2-3.

30 See Psalm 82 and Ephesians 6:12. Both Old and New Testaments envision God battling lesser powers and rebellious angels to bring about the kingdom, implying that the power of free will extends beyond the human race into the "powers" of the universe. For an in-depth modern interpretation of this ancient motif, see Walter Wink, *The Powers That Be* (New York: Doubleday, 1998).

31 1 Timothy 3:16 (KJV).

32 See Gustav Aulen, *Christus Victor: An Historical Study of the Three Main Ideas of Atonement* (Macmillan: New York, 1969). This teaching is summarized by two great hymns: Venantius Honorius Fortunatus, *Pange Lingua* or "Sing My Tongue the Glorious Battle," Hymn 165; and John Henry Neumann, "Praise to the Holiest in the Heights," Hymn 445, both in *The Hymnal*, (New York: The Church Hymnal Corporation, 1982).

33 Luke 23:34. This portrayal of Jesus is especially strong in Luke's Gospel. See Luke's whole version of the passion narrative in Luke 22-23.

34 The ancient hymn *Vexilla Regis*, "The Royal Banners Forward Go" by Fortunatus, Hymn 162 in *The Hymnal* (New York: The Church Hymnal Corporation, 1982).

35 Hebrews 2:14-15.

36 Romans 8:39.

37 Proverbs 1:8–19.

38 Amos 5:19.

39 Proverbs 4:7.

40 See Mark 2:1–12.

41 See Romans 8:20: "[F]or the creation was subjected to futility, not of its own will but by the will of the one who subjected it, in hope." The Greek word *mataiotes* can be translated variously as frustration, vanity, emptiness, futility, purposelessness—human experience of the world when a sense of grace has been lost.

42 Hebrews 2:10.

43 This way of putting it is from Thomas Aquinas, the great medieval theologian, according to his interpreter, the Catholic spiritual writer Baron Friedrich von Hugel: "Aquinas, who teaches the point with emphasis, declares that it is more proper to speak of things that cannot be done, than of God as incapable of doing certain things. . . . He has directly willed Creation, and has deliberately accepted such degree and kind of Self-limitation as this Creation involves." See Baron Friedrich von Hugel, "Suffering and God," in *Essays and Addresses on the Philosophy of Religion, Second Series* (New York: J. M. Dent & Sons Ltd., 1926).

44 Job 42:5.

45 The Hebrew verb *m's* here, sometimes translated "despise myself," is not actually about self-loathing. Job's mind is changed, and he recants his long diatribe against God's justice. The verb can also mean "melt"—the divine epiphany has utterly dissolved Job's previous stance in the world. Job says that he is "undone" or "annihilated." See Marvin Pope, *The Anchor Bible: Job* (Garden City, New York: Doubleday, 1965), 348-49.

46   Exodus 3:12.

47   Main text and alternative variation for Romans 8:28 in the NIV.

48   Abigail Trafford, "After Retirement, a Downturn," *The Washington Post*, May 4, 2004: posted on the Web site Global Action on Aging. Available on the World Wide Web at: http://www.globalaging.org/health/us/2004/downturn.htm

49   Psalm 137:1, 4 (KJV).

50   For further reading, see Win Kayser, *A Glorious Accident: Understanding Our Place in the Cosmic Puzzle* (New York: W. H. Freeman & Co., 1999). This material also exists in videos of an eight-part PBS special of the same name.

51   See Buckminster Fuller with Jerome Agel and Quentin Fiore, *I Seem to Be a Verb* (New York: Bantam, 1970)

52   For further reading about how facts fit into patterns of meaning see Jerome Bruner, *Acts of Meaning* (Cambridge, MA: Harvard University Press, 1990).

53   Frankl observed two kinds of survivors: those who took the path of self-preservation at all costs, and those who held on to their personal philosophy and moral orientation—both frames of meaning. See Viktor Frankl, *Man's Search for Meaning* (Boston: Beacon Press, 1992).

54   See Peter Berger, *The Sacred Canopy: Elements of a Sociological Theory of Religion* (New York: Doubleday, 1967).

55   See Richard Bandler, John Grinder, *Reframing: Neuro-Linguistic Programming and the Transformation of Meaning* (Moab, Utah: Real People Press, 1981) and George Lakoff, Mark Johnson, *Metaphors We Live By* (Chicago: University of Chicago Press, 2nd ed., 2003).

56   Hebrews 4:16.

57   Psalm 88:9, *The Book of Common Prayer* (New York: Church Pension Fund, 1979).

58   For further exploration of Gunilla's insights, see Gunilla Norris, *Being Home: Discovering the Spiritual in the Everyday* (Mahwah, New Jersey: Paulist/ HiddenSpring, 2002).

59   Ephesians 4:13.

60 See Deuteronomy 30:19.

61 Philippians 2:12-13.

62 For stories of angelic rescue, see Martha Beck, *Expecting Adam* (New York: Times Books, 1999); Sophie Burnham, *Book of Angels* (New York: Ballantine, 1990); Billy Graham, *Angels* (Dallas: Word Publications, 1994). Whether one shares the theological framework of the varied and numerous authors of angel rescue books or not, the stories themselves are a powerful witness to spiritual reality.

63 Psalm 18:16-17. Psalm 18 is generally agreed, by conservative and liberal scholars alike, to be from the pen of King David.

64 See Luke's narrative of Jesus' prayer in the Garden of Gethsemane in Luke 22:39–45. "Your desire be done" is my translation. In the Aramaic that Jesus most probably used, the same word can be translated "will" or "desire." Hebrews 5:7 also contains a reference to Gethsemane, with Jesus' "loud cries and tears."

65 See Exodus 3:14. Translations of this verse vary. I am indebted to Rabbi Judah Goldin of Yale University for insight into the multi-faceted meanings of *ehyeh asher ehyeh.*

66 John 3:8.

67 Matthew 5:3, author's translation.

68 See Matthew 6:26–28, 13:33, and 16:15. Also John 7:38, especially in the KJV, which translates the source of this water as the "belly," rather than the "heart" of more modern translations. Hebrew religion believed that spiritual energy flowed through the whole self, flesh and soul alike.

69 Psalm 138:3.

70 God is involved with everyone in the world, guiding and calling each soul step by step into greater truth. As Peter says to Cornelius, the first Gentile convert to the Way of Jesus, "I truly understand that God shows no partiality, but in every nation anyone who fears him and does what is right is acceptable to him" (Acts 10:35). This truth in no way undermines the central Christian affirmation that Jesus Christ is the full revelation of God's way of salvation, and that his life, death, and resurrection

are God's decisive action for the salvation of humanity. Christianity has always taught that there is a "natural revelation" available to all humankind. Furthermore, traditional Catholic doctrine teaches that every person is linked to God through a guardian angel, based on Matthew 18:10: "[T]heir angels continually see the face of my Father in heaven." See Georges Huber, *My Angel Will Go Before You* (Westminster, Maryland: Christian Classics, 1983).

71 See Matthew 6:8.

72 Acts 17:28.

73 For information and instruction on this classical Christian prayer form, see Thomas Keating, *Open Heart, Open Mind: The Contemplative Dimension of the Gospel* (New York: Continuum, reissue 1994).

74 Psalm 46:1.

75 "Thus even though they sustained me by the consolation of woman's milk, neither my mother nor my nurses filled their own breasts but thou, through them, didst give me the food of infancy according to thy ordinance and thy bounty which underlie all things." Augustine of Hippo, *Confessions*, Chapter 6, in Albert Outler, *The Confessions and Enchiridion* (Philadelphia, Westminster Press, 1955), Library of Congress Catalog Card Number: 55-5021. This book is in the public domain. Available from the World Wide Web at: www.fordham.edu/halsall/basis/confessions-bod.html

76 "I am the foundation of your beseeching. First, it is my will that you should have it, and then I make you wish it, and then I make you beseech it." Edmund Collage and James Walsh, trs., *Julian of Norwich: Showings* (New York: Paulist Press, 1978), Short Text, chapter xix, 157. See also Romans 8:26–28.

77 St. Thomas Aquinas, the greatest of the medieval theologians, says that we are naturally inclined to seek God through all the good things in creation until we come to find that goodness in and of itself. Julian of Norwich, the fourteenth-century English, Christian visionary, says that God is "to us everything that is good." *Showings*, Short Text, chapter IV, p. 130.

78 Luke 11:1.

79 "For it is God's will that we do all in our power to preserve our consolation. . . . Therefore it is not God's will that when we feel pain we should pursue it but . . . preserve ourselves in the endless delight of God." *Showings*, Long Text, chapter 15, p. 205.

80 See Matthew 6:7 (KJV), or "meaningless repetition" (NASB).

81 See Isaiah 26:3, which says that a mind "stayed" or "anchored" in God will dwell in "perfect peace," a verse long used to describe the practice of using a repeated prayer-phrase.

82 The repeated choruses of contemporary Christian "praise" music and the harmonious chants of the Taizé community in France are examples of this practice. Information about the Taizé community is available on the World Wide Web at www.taize.fr/en

83 For these exercises, see Ignatius of Loyola, Pierre Wolf, tr., *The Spiritual Exercises* (Ligouri, MO: Ligouri Publications, 1997).

84 The Scriptures abound in images: shepherd, Psalm 23:1, 80:1; king, Psalm 95:3; father, Isaiah 63:16, Matthew 6:9; mother, Isaiah 66:13; light, 1 John 1:5; darkness, Exodus 20:21; rock, Psalm 18:31; water, John 7:38; wind, Acts 2:2; fire, Hebrews 12:29.

85 See Genesis 22:1, Exodus 3:4, 1 Samuel 3:4.

86 Romans 6:13.

87 This is part of what St. Augustine meant by concupiscence, or untamed desire, and is central to Buddhist psychology's analysis of the roots of spiritual suffering.

88 Ephesians 3:20.

89 Lamentations 3:33.

90 Some scholars believe that the manna, or miraculous "bread from heaven" found lying, white and flaky on the desert ground by the children of Israel each morning during their wilderness wanderings (see Exodus 16:13–21), was the white, dried sweet secretion of a bush found on the Sinai peninsula. (*Columbia Encyclopedia*, 6th ed. (New York: Columbia University Press, 2004) available from: World Wide Web: http://www.encyclopedia.com/html/m1/manna.asp

91 The experience of inwardly perceived light is a major motif in mystical experience, sometimes evoked by external light, as was that of the famous Protestant mystic Jacob Boehme, for whom light and fire become major metaphors for God and the human spirit. See Peter Erb, tr., *Jacob Boehme: The Way to Christ* (New York: Paulist Press, 1978).

92 Psalm 27:13 (NKJV).

93 For St. Teresa of Avila, true joy could come only from God and, along with peace, was a sign of the Divine presence. For example, "The devil cannot give this experience because there is so much interior joy in the very intimate part of the soul and so much peace." Kieran Kavanaugh and Otlio Rodriguez, Tr., *Teresa of Avila: The Interior Castle*, 6.9 (New York: Paulist Press, 1979), p. 142.

94 Ecclesiastes 3:1.

95 Ecclesiastes 11:7-8.

96 See Bernard of Morlaix's "Brief life is here our portion." Brief life is here our portion/ Brief sorrow, short lived care/ The life that knows no ending/ The tearless life, is there. Available on the World Wide Web at: http://www.cyberhymnal.org/htm/b/r/brieflif.htm

97 Ecclesiastes 9:10.

98 Matthew 12:36 (KJV).

99 *Gospel of Thomas*, Saying 5, author's translation.

100 Luke 14:31.

101 Psalm 103:14.

102 When Adam fell, God's Son fell. . . . Adam fell from life to death into the valley of this wretched world, and after that into hell. God's Son fell with Adam into the valley of the womb of the maiden who was the fairest daughter of Adam . . . and powerfully he brought him out of hell." Julian of Norwich: *Showings*, Long Text, chapter 51, 267–78.

103 See Luke 6:45.

104 John 1:5.

105 Psalm 56:3.

106 John 16:22.

107 John 11:35 (KJV).

108 For recent medical research on social support and physical resilience, see Dean Ornish, *Love and Survival: The Scientific Basis for the Healing Power of Intimacy* (New York: HarperCollins, 1998).

109 Psalm 69:20 Handel's Messiah Libretto. See comments in text.

110 This well-known tale of the Buddha is paralleled by St. Paul's saying that "if one member suffers, all suffer" (1 Corinthians 12:26).

111 I am indebted for this phrase to the teaching of Tilden Edwards, founder of the Shalem Institute for Spiritual Formation in Bethesda, Maryland, under whom I studied spiritual direction. For further reading in his wisdom see Tilden Edwards, *Living in the Presence: Spiritual Exercises to Open Your Life to the Awareness of God* (San Francisco: HarperSanFrancisco, 1994.)

112 See 1 Corinthians 5:3-4.

113 "The Royal Banners Forward Go," cited above, note 34.

114 The New Testament tells us that Jesus was not just raised from the dead, but also "brought life and immortality to light through the gospel," (2 Timothy 1:9-10). Jesus' resurrection manifests a deeper reality in the pattern of God's own life. The idea that Jesus "manifested the resurrection" is a regular feature of Eastern Orthodox prayers, as in Great Vespers for Saturday evening: "Accept our evening prayers, O holy Lord . . . for You a l o n e manifested the resurrection to the world." Byzantine Catholic Church in America Faith & Worship: *Vespers.*
Available from the World Wide Web at :
http://www.byzcath.org/faith/worship/vespers-saturday-evenings.html

115 See Psalm 139:24-25, *1928 Book of Common Prayer* (New York: Church Pension Fund, 1945).

116 Paraphrase of Mark 1:11.

117 This biblical motif takes on added meaning by the modern discovery of a stratum of chaos underlying the ordered world of Newtonian physics. The "ordered disorder" of chaos supports

and births the "ordered order" of the world of regular physical reality.

118 John 5:17.

119 Gerard Manley Hopkins, "God's Grandeur," can be found in Stephen Mitchell, *The Enlightened Heart* (New York: Harper & Row, 1989). The poem itself is in the public domain.

120 See Psalm 85:10, Amos 5:24, Isaiah 11:9.

121 See Romans 8:23 and 2 Corinthians 6:1 (NIV).

122 As the Lord's Prayer makes clear, the kingdom of which Jesus speaks is meant to come "on earth," not just "in heaven" (Matthew 6:10). From Genesis to Revelation, the Bible is the story of God's patient working to call human beings to be citizens of this heaven-directed realization of God's will for this planet's life. Even the saints in heaven pray for this kingdom to come (see Revelation 6:10).

123 2 Peter 1:4 (NKJV). Paul even dares to say that we are called to complete "what is lacking in Christ's afflictions" (Colossians 1:24). In whatever sense the work of Christ is "finished" on the cross, its mediation to the world, for Paul, continues to be necessary—one aspect of our God-given privilege of participating in the divine nature.

124 James 5:16 (KJV).

125 "Again, truly I tell you, if two of you agree on earth about any thing you ask, it will be done for you by my Father in heaven." See Matthew 18:19.

126 Luke 13:4.

127 Christopher Fry, *A Sleep of Prisoners* (New York: Oxford University Press, 1951).

128 The Scriptures are clear, to me, that the need for prayer continues beyond physical death, for they picture the saints praying for the needs of the world in heaven, crying out, "How long, O Lord," until the kingdom fully comes. (Revelation 6:10, KJV)

129 Belief about how long the divine Love persists in seeking those who refuse it have differed in Christianity through the centuries,

some believing, that after death there are no further opportunities for repentance, others, as I do, that God's love will persist in seeking to redeem even the most recalcitrant soul. My belief is rooted in Jesus' statement that God's love is like a shepherd who seeks the lost sheep "until he finds it" (Luke 15:4), as well as in the passage in 1 Peter about Christ seeking the "souls in prison" who had disobeyed during the flood (1 Peter 3:19-20). See C. S. Lewis's discussion of the afterlife in *The Great Divorce* (New York, MacMillan, 1946).

130 Robert Corin Morris, 1999, inspired by Piero della Francesca's fresco *Resurrection*. The "mothering Dark" of the poem, which I see in Christ's eyes in that painting, is an evocation of the "dazzling darkness" spoken of by Christian mystics, the dark unknownness of God out of which arises the first light of creation.

130 Robert Corin Morris, 1999, inspired by Piero della Francesca's fresco *Resurrection*. The "mothering Dark" of the poem, which I see in Christ's eyes in that painting, is an evocation of the "dazzling darkness" spoken of by Christian mystics, the dark unknownness of God out of which arises the first light of creation.

131 Psalm 103:1–6.

ABOUT PARACLETE PRESS

WHO WE ARE

Paraclete Press is an ecumenical publisher of books on Christian spirituality for people of all denominations and backgrounds.

We publish books that represent the wide spectrum of Christian belief and practice—Catholic, Orthodox and Protestant.

We market our books primarily through booksellers; we are what is called a "trade" publisher, which means that we like it best when readers buy our books from booksellers, our partners in successfully reaching as wide an audience as possible.

We are uniquely positioned in the marketplace without connection to a large corporation or conglomerate and with informal relationships to many branches and denominations of faith, rather than a formal relationship to any single one. We focus on publishing a diversity of thoughts and perspectives—the fruit of our diversity as a company.

WHAT WE ARE DOING

Paraclete Press is publishing books that show the diversity and depth of what it means to be Christian. We publish books that reflect the Christian experience across many cultures, time periods, and houses of worship.

We publish books about spiritual practice, history, ideas, customs, and rituals, and books that nourish the vibrant life of the church.

We have several different series of books within Paraclete Press, including the bestselling Living Library series of modernized classic texts, A Voice from the Monastery giving voice to men and women monastics on what it means to live a spiritual life today, and Many Mansions—for exploring the riches of the world's religious traditions and discovering how other faiths inform Christian thought and practice.

Learn more about us at our website:
www.paracletepress.com, or call us toll-free at
1-800-451-5006.